CHRISTIAN HEROES: THEN & NOW

NORMAN GRUBB

Mission Builder

CHRISTIAN HEROES: THEN & NOW

NORMAN GRUBB

Mission Builder

JANET & GEOFF BENGE

YWAM
PUBLISHING
P.O. BOX 55787 SEATTLE, WA 98155

YWAM Publishing is the publishing ministry of Youth With A Mission (YWAM), an international missionary organization of Christians from many denominations dedicated to presenting Jesus Christ to this generation. To this end, YWAM has focused its efforts in three main areas: (1) training and equipping believers for their part in fulfilling the Great Commission (Matthew 28:19), (2) personal evangelism, and (3) mercy ministry (medical and relief work).

For a free catalog of books and materials, call (425) 771-1153 or (800) 922-2143. Visit us online at www.ywampublishing.com.

Norman Grubb: Mission Builder

Published by YWAM Publishing
a ministry of Youth With A Mission
P.O. Box 55787, Seattle, WA 98155-0787

ISBN 978-1-57658-915-1 (paperback)
ISBN 978-1-57658-655-6 (e-book)

First printing 2019

Printed in the United States of America

CHRISTIAN HEROES: THEN & NOW

Available in paperback, e-book, and audiobook formats.
Unit Study Curriculum Guides are available for select biographies.
www.HeroesThenAndNow.com

Northern Belgian Congo
(Dem. Rep. of the Congo)

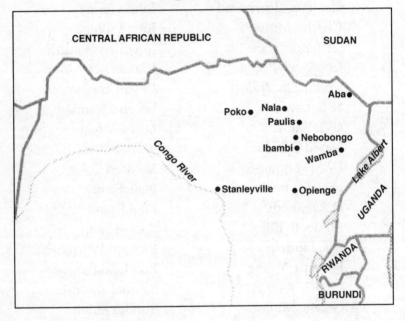

Contents

Chapter 1

A Blighty

For Norman Grubb and his men, it was zero hour. "Over the top!" Norman ordered, then turned to climb one of the ladders leading up to the lip of the trench. Scrambling from the trench, he surged forward with his platoon, rifles in front, bayonets attached. Within seconds, withering German machine-gun fire cut horizontally across the battlefield. Norman watched as fellow soldiers around him collapsed facedown in the mud. Others advanced toward their target. After crossing a stream, the men took shelter from machine-gun fire and incoming mortar shells by crouching behind decimated trees or jumping into shell craters from previous battles. Norman took cover in a shell crater with a young private.

Another blast of gunfire erupted. Norman watched as the private next to him slumped backward dead. As he tried to assess the situation around him, Norman felt a stinging thump on the back of his right leg. He looked down and saw blood pulsing from a wound. A machine-gun bullet had passed through his leg above the knee. Norman knew he couldn't fight on. He needed urgent medical attention. Using the dead private's rifle as a crutch, he stumbled out of the crater and back toward Allied lines. As he moved, a soldier heading out into the rain of machine-gun bullets yelled, "Lucky Grubb! He's got a blighty!" A blighty was a wound severe enough to take a soldier out of action but hopefully not serious enough to kill him. At that moment Norman didn't feel so lucky.

One painful step after another, Norman made his way toward a first-aid dugout, where his leg was tightly bandaged. He was then lifted into an ambulance with several other men and driven to a makeshift military hospital behind the Western Front. Within a day, Norman was aboard a hospital ship on his way back to England.

In England Norman was transferred to the 5th Northern General Hospital in Leicester, a military hospital set up in several large rectangular, red-brick buildings that had once been a mental asylum. Inside, Norman was assigned a metal-frame bed with a kapok mattress and neatly folded sheets. Since he couldn't walk, two orderlies lifted him into bed. Its comfort was something he could only dream about when he was in the trenches in France.

Days passed slowly at the 5th Northern General Hospital. Everyone in Norman's ward eagerly awaited the arrival of new patients in the hope they had up-to-date news from the battlefront.

On Norman's third day in the hospital, a tall man who looked to be about ten years older than Norman walked slowly through the ward. The man, who wore a clerical collar, stopped at each bed to talk with its wounded occupant.

"Good afternoon. How are you? I'm Reverend Gilbert Barclay," the man said when he reached Norman.

Pulling himself to a sitting position, Norman replied, "Glad to meet you, Padre."

"Is there anything I can do for you or pray for you today?" Gilbert asked.

Norman sensed that the man had a genuine faith, and soon the two of them were deep in conversation. Gilbert served as a chaplain to the wounded soldiers at the 5th Northern General Hospital. He was also a Church of England clergyman and pastor of a church in Carlisle, to the north. Norman eagerly told him how his father was a Church of England clergyman in Poole. As the two continued talking, Norman realized that one of his father's aunts lived in Carlisle. Gilbert informed him that he knew her well and that she was an active member of his parish.

When Gilbert moved on to talk to the next wounded soldier, Norman knew he'd made a friend. Little did he know that this new friendship would change the course of his life.

Chapter 2

South Lodge

Norman stared at the fishing boats bobbing at anchor in the inner harbor. Moments later he heard the train's brakes squeal as they began slowing and Lowestoft Railway Station came into view. The station looked like most of the other stations the train had stopped at on the 130-mile trip from Oxton.

"Lowestoft! Lowestoft!" the conductor announced as he walked through the carriage. Norman was already on his feet. He wore the uniform of his new school, South Lodge. He grabbed his cap, pulled down his suitcase from the overhead luggage rack, and followed several other passengers leaving the train. Out on the station platform he set down his suitcase and looked around. His mother had told him to wait for someone from South Lodge School to come

13

for him. Before all the passengers had disembarked the train, a tall man with a black moustache waved at Norman. "Might you be young Master Grubb?" he inquired as he got closer.

"Yes, sir," Norman said with a nod.

"Well," said the mustachioed man. "I'm Arthur Phillips. The boys at school call me Mr. Arthur. Do you have everything?"

"Yes," Norman said.

"The school's a half mile away. It's a pleasant walk south along the waterfront," Mr. Arthur said as the two set off toward a nearby bridge. "We're crossing over the entrance to Lowestoft Harbor. Lowestoft is a major fishing port, and the harbor has mooring for a thousand boats," Mr. Arthur said as they walked. "And do you know what that is?" he asked, pointing to a piece of land jutting into the ocean just north of them.

Norman studied the rocky promontory.

"That's Lowestoft Ness, the most easterly point in the United Kingdom. Head east from here across the North Sea and what's the nearest country you will come to?" Mr. Arthur asked.

Squinting against the afternoon sun as he looked out across the sea, Norman thought for a few moments before saying, "Holland?"

"Quite right, lad, just 110 miles straight across. The closeness accounts for the railhead here in Lowestoft and the busy docks as ships ply between the two countries."

Norman nodded. He sensed he was going to learn a lot of history and geography at his new school.

Once across the bridge, the two of them walked south along the esplanade. They crossed Claremont Road as it bisected the esplanade and continued south a short distance until Mr. Arthur turned into the courtyard beside a sturdy three-story red-brick building with large bay windows on the front two stories. "Here we are at South Lodge, your home for the next five years," Mr. Arthur said. And pointing across the street he added, "Now, isn't that some view?"

Norman looked across the street. Beyond some low sand dunes, the expansive blue ocean was dotted with whitecaps to the horizon, the shoreline broken only by a small pier that stretched out into the water from the beach. Despite the wonderful view, Norman forced back tears. It seemed impossible for him to imagine living in this place until he was fourteen years old. He already missed his family, and Lowestoft was nothing like the beautiful village of Oxton away to the northwest in Nottinghamshire, where Norman had lived since the age of two.

Over the next few days Norman settled into his dormitory room at South Lodge School and got used to eating the stodgy food served in the dining room, keeping up with the tight schedule and being constantly surrounded by other boys his own age. Until now, he hadn't attended a proper school. In addition to employing two maids, a gardener, and a houseboy to tend to the family, Norman's father, the vicar of St. Peter & St. Paul's Church Oxton, had hired a governess to teach Norman and his siblings. Like Norman, Miss Turner, the governess, loved nature and allowed him, his younger brother, Kenneth, and his younger sister, Violet, to wander nearby Sherwood Forest. It was the place where the legendary folklore hero Robin Hood and his band of followers were said to have lived and roamed.

Now, instead of being free to enjoy the expansiveness of Sherwood Forest, Norman was caged inside a red-brick school building. None of the students were allowed to be outside without permission, and when they did go out, they normally walked two by two in a long line to the sports fields, a few minutes away. Sports became the highlight of Norman's day. Since South Lodge School had only fifty students, it wasn't difficult for Norman to imagine one day making the school's top teams in hockey, rugby, and cricket, the three traditional English schoolboy sports. Norman liked rugby best, and while not a large boy, he was fast on his feet and soon earned a reputation for dodging the other team's defense. Yet even with sports, days at South Lodge moved slowly for Norman, especially as winter approached and the nor'easters roared in from the North Sea accompanied by bitter cold winds. No amount of layered clothing seemed to keep him warm against the biting wind.

Norman checked off each day on the calendar, yearning for holidays and school breaks when he could go home to Oxton. As the days passed, he slowly adjusted to the rhythm of the school. He studied Latin, Greek, English literature, and mathematics, along with the Bible. Each morning the Reverend Richard Phillips, principal of South Lodge School and Mr. Arthur's brother, held a chapel service at which each boy in the school was given the same verse of Scripture to memorize. By the end of the first term, they had all memorized an entire chapter of the Bible, which each boy recited aloud to the rest of the school. Norman found it easy to learn Bible verses. Back home in Oxton, his father had often quoted Bible passages to Norman and explained their meaning.

The first term at South Lodge lasted twelve weeks, after which Norman returned to Oxton for the Christmas holiday. Norman was delighted to see his family again. His father, the Reverend Harry Grubb, was fifty-five years old, much older than most of the fathers of the other boys in Norman's class. By now he was mostly bald, with a fringe of white hair around the sides of his head. Although Norman loved his father, he did find it difficult to talk to him about everyday things. His father was from a wealthy Irish family that had lost their fortune in a bad business deal. Before that happened, Mr. Grubb had attended Trinity College, Dublin, the top university in Ireland. From there he'd gone on to Europe to study. He was a Hebrew scholar who, along with Hebrew and English, spoke fluent German and French. He also loved poetry.

Norman, on the other hand, had little time for poetry or foreign languages and found it much easier to relate to his mother. Margaret Grubb also came from a wealthy family and was related to many lords and ladies, though it was easy for Norman to forget that when he was with her. At forty years of age, she was much younger than Norman's father, and she loved organizing outings for the Grubb children and other young people in the village.

The first time he arrived back in Oxton from South Lodge School, Norman was surprised to learn that his parents had taken in two small children, Cecil and Gladys Price, to live with them. Cecil and Gladys's parents were friends of Norman's mother and father and were serving as missionaries in central India. Since it had been deemed too dangerous for the Prices' children to accompany them, it was arranged that they would stay behind in England with the Grubbs. Cecil and Gladys quickly adapted to their new life, and by the end of the Christmas holiday, Norman looked upon them as part of the family.

Christmas break passed quickly, and before Norman knew it, he was on the train headed back to Lowestoft and the life of a public-school boy.

Back at South Lodge, Norman readjusted. By now he realized he was far from being the most popular student. In fact, he'd earned a reputation for being a tattletale, which Norman soon discovered had its risks. One day several boys swooped in and grabbed him before he could escape. Norman tried to struggle, but the other boys had a firm grip on him. A few moments later they had dragged him to the school basement, where they threw him into a coal bunker. "You're not going to tell on anyone from in there," one of the boys snarled as he closed the door with Norman inside.

Alone in the pitch black of the coal bunker, Norman was terrified. He screamed louder than he'd

ever screamed before as he kicked at the bunker
door. After what seemed an eternity, the bunker door
swung open, and Mr. Arthur poked his head in to
see what the trouble was. Norman was hoarse from
screaming, and tears streaked his coal-dusted cheeks
as he emerged from the bunker, eager to tell Mr.
Arthur who it was that had bundled him into the coal
bunker against his will.

Mr. Arthur talked to the boys Norman mentioned
and then barked, "Bird, go up to the Bow Room!"

At the sound of these words, Norman felt pangs
of guilt for what John Bird was about to endure. The
feeling surprised him. He'd thought punishment for
the ring leader of the attack would make him feel
happy and vindicated. But it didn't. He felt quite the
opposite.

As was the custom at South Lodge, Norman, after
washing the coal dust from his face, joined the other
students as they stood and listened in the corridor
below the Bow Room, a large dormitory room above
with a bow window at one end. While the voice of
Arthur Phillips was muffled, all the boys knew what
was happening. Mr. Arthur was pointing out matter-
of-factly what rule John Bird had broken and was asking him to bend over and hold his ankles. Moments
later the unmistakable crack of a cane against soft
flesh reverberated through the corridor. It was followed by another crack and then another, until six
strokes of the cane had been administered as punishment for instigating the attack on Norman. The boys
could hear John groan in the room above.

Normally after punishment, the student who had been caned went down to the basement lavatory, where he showed a few chosen friends what the cane had done to his backside. On this occasion, John asked for Norman to be one of those who came down to view the result of the caning. Norman found himself shaking as he stared at the wound. Large, bright-red horizontal welts stretched across John's buttocks, and already the edges of the welts showed the black-and-blue signs of bruising. Norman felt a knot in the pit of his stomach as he confronted the physical reality of what his tattling on another student had wrought. He was even more shaken when Mr. Arthur took him aside and told Norman he never wanted to hear him scream like that again and get other boys into trouble. If he did so, he assured Norman that he also would be sent to the Bow Room for punishment. That was it for Norman. Right there and then he decided he would never be a tattletale. Nobody would hear a peep from him ever again.

One year in Lowestoft went by, and then another, and with their passing, a pattern was established for Norman. Twelve weeks at school would be followed by two or three weeks at home, and then it was back to Lowestoft for the next term. Even though Norman was not particularly interested in schoolwork, he didn't want to disappoint his parents and so worked hard to keep up his grades. By the time he graduated from South Lodge in 1909 he was the top student in the school. Not surprisingly, he had also made the first team in cricket, rugby, and hockey.

As Norman's time at South Lodge school drew to a close, the question of where he would attend high school loomed large. Although both of Norman's parents came from well-off families, they lived on a low income, which would stretch only so far, especially with six children to care for. Norman's older brother, Harold, was already a boarder at Haileybury College, but it was unlikely the family had the money to send all of their children there. As he pondered where he might end up at high school, Norman learned that Mr. Phillips had applied for a scholarship on his behalf to attend Marlborough College, one of the best traditional boarding schools for boys in England. The college awarded fifteen scholarships each year to the sons of Church of England clergymen like Norman. Norman and his parents were delighted when they learned he had won a place at Marlborough College. He was set to begin school there in autumn 1909, and that summer Norman was anxious about what lay ahead for him.

Chapter 3

An Odd Thought Struck Him

In autumn 1909, Norman found himself alone at the start of another school year. Norman thought he knew all about boarding school, but he still found it hard to adjust to life at Marlborough College. This time, instead of fifty boys in the school there were six hundred, all divided into "houses," within which they studied together, shared dormitories, ate in the dining hall, and were divided into sports teams.

Norman hoped to fit in by becoming a "blood," as the Marlborough College students dubbed the top sports players. It would be a tough fight to get there, but Norman was determined to practice constantly until he was good enough.

At the beginning of Norman's second year at Marlborough College, he had his first opportunity to

23

be a leader. It was the fourth and last term he would be in A House, and he was made a dormitory captain. Like other public schools in England, Marlborough College had many traditions. One of these allowed a dormitory captain to punish the students under his authority. The punishment was a spanking on the bottom with a sports shoe. And when a dormitory captain was promoted to prefect, he could hit his charges with a cane. One Saturday, Norman became frustrated with his dormitory of new boys. He couldn't make the students show him the level of respect he thought he deserved. He lined them up and hit each boy, including his deputy dormitory captain, with a sports shoe. Although he had the right to do this, the boys under him were incensed by his action and plotted revenge.

During the day the boys used outdoor toilets, or privies, but at night in their dormitory, no one was allowed outside. Instead, under each bed was a chamber pot, which the boys could use as a toilet if needed. The youngest boys emptied and cleaned all the chamber pots in the morning. The cleaned pots were then placed back into a wire cage beside the line of porcelain basins the boys used for washing their hands and face.

Early one Sunday morning Norman awoke with a vague feeling he was being watched. He opened his eyes, and sure enough his bed was surrounded by the boys he'd beaten with a sports shoe earlier. Norman immediately yelled "Turf!" This was another custom at Marlborough College whereby the most senior boy in a room had the right to sit or lie where he liked, and if another boy was already there, he had to vacate the spot for the senior boy. As Norman yelled "Turf," one of the boys laughed and informed him it was not yet eight o'clock in the morning. Norman's heart sank. He had forgotten that the rule could not be invoked until after that time.

Instead of backing away from Norman, the boys pulled off his blankets and dragged him out of bed. Norman tried to struggle, then gave up—he was outnumbered fifteen to one. The boys carried him to the end of the dorm. As they hoisted him onto the long wash table, Norman heard the door to the chamber pots cage rattle open. He then felt himself being heaved into the cage and heard the door click shut behind him.

The dorm boys stood around the cage mocking Norman. It was only 7:00 a.m., and he was forced to sit for an hour listening to their ridicule until eight o'clock, when he could call "Turf" and demand to be released. It was one of the longest hours of Norman's life. When the ordeal was over, he still had to go to breakfast in the dining hall and watch as news spread that the captain of A House dorm had been locked up by his own boys.

Norman was glad at the end of his fourth term to be done with A House. From there he chose to go into C3 House, where he would stay for the rest of his time at Marlborough College.

At college, nothing thrilled Norman more than playing rugby, and a match was held most Saturdays during winter. He found the best position for him on a team was fullback. In that position it was his job to tackle below the knees the opposing players running at him with the ball and bring them to the ground. And when the ball was kicked forward by the opposing team, he had to chase it down and fall on it, creating a ruck from which his team would hopefully win possession of the ball. As he worked hard to improve his performance, things looked hopeful that Norman would one day wear the blue-and-white striped jersey and blue knickerbockers of players in the first fifteen, the college's top rugby team.

By September 1912, seventeen-year-old Norman looked as though he was well on the way to achieving his rugby dream. The C3 House team he played for had a poor reputation and often finished at the bottom of local interschool rugby. But when Philip Margetson became the new captain of the team, things began to change. He inspired the other team members to play harder than they had ever played before. And their effort paid off when, instead of finishing at the bottom of the interschool competition, they finished at the top, allowing them to challenge the reigning rugby squad in the district, the Sandford Street Boys School team from nearby Swindon.

Although the Sandford Street Boys School rugby team was the clear favorite to win the match, a large crowd showed up to watch the game. As he had done all season, Captain Margetson inspired the C3 House rugby team members to give the game their all. At fullback, Norman rose to the occasion, tackling

Sandford players as they tried to breakthrough C3's defenses, catching the ball, and kicking it away or falling on it to form a ruck when he needed to. He played his heart out, and to his amazement the C3 team led for a more than half the game. When the final whistle blew, the team had been only narrowly beaten by what was supposed to be the far superior team. As Norman walked from the field at the end of the game, he was proud of his performance at fullback.

Other boys told him they were impressed by his performance. A week later the house captains at Marlborough College voted on the teams that would represent the entire school, and Norman was elated to be picked for the second team. The honor allowed him to wear a special sports uniform that included a dark blue cap with silver tassels. Norman had reached what was known at Marlborough as "minor blood" status. His ambition of playing for the college's top team was well under way.

The next year went even better for Norman. His father became vicar at St. Paul's Church in Poole on the south coast of England. Norman enjoyed spending his summer vacation there with the family. Poole was much larger than Oxton and had many more interesting things to see and explore.

Once back at Marlborough College after summer break, Norman at last enjoyed the respect of the other boys and joined the O.T.C. (Officer's Training Corps), where he learned to shoot a rifle and march in formation. By now he and most of the population of Great Britain were aware that O.T.C. training was not just an exercise to keep school-age young men fit and occupied. Several European nations, including Great Britain, had sprawling colonies scattered around the world. Soldiers were being deployed to some of those far-flung places to settle violent disputes. At the same time as imperial rivals in Africa competed to exploit the continent's resources, Britain and France became suspicious that Germany was trying to get its hands on some of those resources. It was obvious to the British that more troops were necessary to maintain the established colonial order in Africa. As well, peace was fraying in the Balkans region of southeastern Europe, where fighting had crushed the control of the Ottoman Empire. Now newly liberated Serbia wanted to unite all Slavic people in the area, which put pressure on the power of the Austro-Hungarian Empire in the region. The Russian Empire supported Serbia, while Germany backed Austria's opposition to Serbia's desire to unite.

While peace and stability were threatened in Europe and some of the colonies, Norman was sure that politicians and diplomats would eventually sort out such difficulties without resorting to war. For now, he was in his last year at Marlborough College and had everything he wanted. He was House Captain for C3, and he was quite sure he would be given the position of fullback in the first fifteen rugby team. And he'd put in enough academic work to be in the top twenty students at school, though he wasn't interested in pushing himself to be the best.

At the official trials game for the first fifteen rugby team, the hopeful students took turns playing against their teachers, or "beaks," as they called them. With his usual verve, Norman tackled anyone with the ball who came near him and punted it downfield over the heads of the beaks when it was kicked his way. During the second half of the game, while Norman was punting the ball, he was tackled by the burliest teacher, Master Stagg.

Norman felt his right leg twist as he crashed to the ground. After he was tackled, he lay on the playing field unable to get up. Several teachers skilled in first aid looked him over, after which Norman was lifted onto a stretcher and carried to the college infirmary, where a doctor examined him and announced that Norman had torn the cartilage in his knee. Not only would he be unable to play rugby for the rest of the season, but also he would have to undergo surgery to repair the tear.

Neither of these was part of Norman's plan for his life, and he was feeling bitter by the time the surgery was over. He spent days convalescing in the hospital, using some of that time going over the things that had recently gone wrong in his life. Then one day, an odd thought struck him: was he being self-centered? Why did he expect everything to revolve around him? Why did everything have to work out just the way he wanted?

Norman thought back over his life. Everyone had always been there to help make his life easier. His mother doted on him, his father supplied him with everything he needed for boarding school, and Norman expected all of that and more. Now, for the first time, he wondered if that was really all there was to life: getting people to do things for you to make your life easier. It certainly didn't feel very meaningful, and he asked himself what *would* be meaningful? And where did the God he'd learned about at home and school fit in? Was Jesus really an historic figure or just the result of some early writer's active imagination?

Fully recovered from his knee surgery, Norman still hadn't found answers to his questions when he returned home from college for Easter break at the beginning of April 1914. Spring was early, and the weather in Poole was unusually warm. During the break, Norman and his older brother Harold spent a lot of time playing tennis at the home of Major Gartside-Tippinge and his wife, who were friends of their parents. The couple lived in a large house that had an immaculately mowed tennis court. When the boys played tennis, however, they were always leery of starting a conversation with either of their hosts, who were enthusiastic Christians. Mrs. Gartside-Tippinge's brother was general director of China Inland Mission, which the British missionary Hudson Taylor had started. Both boys were careful to avoid personal conversations with the major whenever they could. One day, however, Major Gartside-Tippinge cornered Norman in the drawing room just as he watched Harold slip away out the side door. Norman took a deep breath as the major spoke.

"You know, Norman, you're a fine boy. How old are you now?"

"Eighteen, sir," Norman replied.

"Well, I'm sure you have a bright future ahead of you, but I have to ask you, does that future include Christ Jesus? Do you belong to Christ?"

Norman felt his face turn bright red. He was used to hearing about Jesus Christ in the formal setting of church. He'd been confirmed into the Church of England two years before. He knew all the correct prayers and catechisms, but did he belong to Christ? That was the kind of personal question he did not want to answer. Lowering his head, he mumbled something about being born in a Christian home and going to chapel every morning at school since he was nine years old.

"But there is more," Major Gartside-Tippinge said. "I think you need to kneel right now and pray that God will reveal Himself to you. You shouldn't wait one minute more to give yourself to Christ."

Norman knew he was trapped. He was, after all, the son of a vicar, and he could hardly refuse to pray without it becoming a scene. He knelt down and mumbled a few words. As soon as he could, Norman wrapped up his prayer with a loud "Amen," stood up, thanked the major for his hospitality, and fled the Gartside-Tippinges' home.

Taking a tram back to the vicarage, Norman tried to get Major Gartside-Tippinge's words out of his mind. But he couldn't. Was he really a Christian, or did he just know how to act like one? Deep down this question stirred within Norman. He knew the answer. He'd thought of God as a lucky charm, something to have around if things went wrong. But had he ever surrendered his life to God? He knew the answer to that question too—no, he had not.

As soon as he got home, Norman rushed upstairs to his bedroom, got down on his knees, and asked God to forgive his sins and make him a new person inside. Immediately, he felt a wave of joy wash over him. He didn't have to worry anymore. He belonged to God—for all eternity.

Norman half expected to feel deflated when he awoke the next morning. The English school system discouraged emotional outbursts, and he had gone to bed feeling almost too excited to sleep. But the feeling was still there when he woke, along with the assurance that something important had happened to him.

When he returned to Marlborough College after Easter break, Norman told his closest friends about his newfound faith. One of them, Henry de Condole, was astonished. "If that's what real Christianity is about, then none of us have it!" he said. Norman understood what he meant. Somehow, he and most of the boys he knew at school were so steeped in church services and chapel times that they had ignored the message being preached.

During his last term at Marlborough, Norman and most of his friends assumed that in the autumn they would be off to university—hopefully either Oxford or Cambridge—and then on to a distinguished career somewhere. Norman sat his university entrance exams and was delighted to be awarded a scholarship to Sidney Sussex College at Cambridge. But before he could get there, events in Europe overcame Great Britain.

On June 28, 1914, Archduke Franz Ferdinand of Austria and his wife, Sophie, Duchess of Hohenberg, were shot dead in Sarajevo by assassin Gavrilo Princip, a Bosnian Serb and member of an organization seeking to end the Austro-Hungarian rule of his country. Archduke Ferdinand was heir to the Austro-Hungarian throne, and his assassination threw Europe into turmoil, triggering a chain of events that eventually led countries of Europe into war with each other.

On August 4, 1914, Germany invaded neutral Belgium. In response, that same day, Great Britain declared war on Germany. As a loyal Englishman, Norman's path was set. Duty called. He would become a soldier, not a scholar.

Norman filled out the application forms for enrollment in the army and waited for a commission. He was staying with his parents in Poole at the time, and while there, his older brother Harold left for the war. It was a proud moment for the Grubb family, and Norman could hardly wait to join his brother on the battlefront. In the meantime, freshly liberated from an all-boys boarding school, Norman discovered girls—or more precisely one girl in particular.

Chapter 4

Second Lieutenant

Eleanor lived in nearby Bournemouth. Although she was four years older than Norman, the two became instant friends, then boyfriend and girlfriend. Norman loved spending time with Eleanor, and they enjoyed long conversations as they walked beside the Bourne River. Both knew the relationship was unlikely to become long-term because of the war, yet Norman was delighted to be in the company of a young woman. He particularly liked telling Eleanor about his newfound faith, though he noticed she seemed puzzled as to how someone could be as enthusiastic about God as he was. Nonetheless, she was a good listener.

At the same time Norman was dating Eleanor, his favorite uncle, the Reverend George Grubb, his father's brother, came to visit the family. Norman's father, Harry, came from an old Irish Quaker family with eleven children, nine of whom were still alive. Although Norman's grandfather, had been dismissed from his Quaker meeting for dancing and going to concerts, several of his children, including Norman's father and Uncle George, had a vibrant Christian faith. Uncle George was often one of the main speakers at the large Keswick Convention held each summer in Northwestern England, and he traveled the world as an evangelist.

During George Grubb's visit, Norman enjoyed long talks with him over cups of tea. Norman told his uncle all about Eleanor, and in response Uncle George gave him a copy of a booklet about being completely dedicated to God. Norman began reading the booklet one evening after dinner. Before he got to the end of the first page, he threw the booklet to the floor. "What does that author know?" he muttered as he stared at the wall. The words that stung him on the first page were about how a Christian cannot have Christ at the heart of all things and love someone who does not have the same passion for Christ. He thought of Eleanor. He wondered what kind of God would require him to give up someone as nice as her. He tried over and over to justify his relationship with Eleanor, but deep in his heart he knew the words he'd read in the booklet were right. He should not be going out with someone who didn't share his love for God. Of course, knowing this and doing something about it were two very different things.

After wrestling for several weeks with the notion of breaking up with Eleanor, Norman felt miserable. He knew the only way out of his misery was to tell her he could no longer see her. Eleanor was aghast at the news, accusing Norman of being a religious fanatic. While this hurt Norman deeply, he felt he'd passed a big test in his Christian journey.

A week after breaking up with Eleanor, Norman received his army enlistment papers. Because he had attended a private boarding school and been in the O.T.C. he was commissioned with the rank of second lieutenant in the 9th Battalion of the Gloucester Regiment. Norman felt exhilarated holding the papers in his hands. As second lieutenant he would be in command of a platoon of soldiers numbering up to about forty-five men.

On September 14, 1914, Second Lieutenant Norman Grubb stood to attention in front of his platoon, a motley group of forty men, most of whom were older than him and much less educated. When Lord Kitchener, the British Secretary of State for War, appealed for 100,000 men to volunteer to take up arms and fight in the war, three-quarters of a million men lined up to apply, overwhelming recruitment centers at police stations and courthouses. Those volunteers who were working-class men and had left school at age twelve were assigned as foot soldiers, while any man who had been through the British public high school system or university was automatically given a higher rank.

Norman inspected the men of his platoon their first day at Codford Training Camp nestled on undulating

Salisbury Plain in southern England. Virtually all of the men had more life experience than he had, and many had practical skills that Norman's education hadn't included. Norman had the better schooling, but education wasn't something the soldiers particularly respected. Norman knew it would be hard for the men to work under his leadership, but according to his commander, they would have one year of intense training in England before being shipped off to live or die together on the battlefield. Somehow, they would all have to learn to trust each other.

Norman and his platoon were considered lucky to be training at Codford Camp. Many other training camps were made up of row after row of tents, but Codford had wooden huts for the enlisted men. Norman and the other officers were billeted in private homes nearby. It was difficult to train the men for real combat. Many of them had never handled a rifle, and because of acute shortages, they were issued dummy wooden rifles and told to imagine they were real. As an officer, Norman purchased his own uniform, but the men under him had to train in their own clothes, since no khaki uniforms were yet available for them.

Life soon fell into a pattern for Norman, a pattern he had no trouble adjusting to. He'd spent the past ten years living with other boys, eating together, wearing a uniform, and obeying the orders of his schoolmasters. The military training camp wasn't that different in many respects. The day started at 5:30 a.m. with reveille. An hour later the officers arrived to supervise morning parade and fitness exercises. Then it was breakfast, followed by three hours of drills, where the men practiced route marching, learned to handle and take care of their dummy rifles and bayonets to get ready for the time they would be replaced with real ones, and generally adjusted to army life and discipline.

Norman and his platoon had been training at Codford Training Camp for three months when their training took on new urgency. On December 16, 1914, the German Imperial Navy bombarded three towns, Whitby, Hartlepool, and Scarborough, all located along the Yorkshire coast of northern England, killing 137 civilians and wounding 455. The attack was the first time that Germans had killed anyone on British soil, and it was a sobering reminder to Norman and his men of what was at stake in the war raging in Europe.

From reading the newspapers and listening to reports from various superior officers, Norman kept abreast of developments in the fighting. Following the outbreak of war in August, after invading Belgium and Luxembourg, the German army swept into eastern France, occupying several important French industrial regions. For a while it looked as if the Germans might overrun Paris too. They were forty-three miles from the French capital when British and French troops managed to counterattack and stop the German advance. In the face of the attack, the Germans retreated eastward until the two opposing sides had dug a series of long, meandering fortified trenches stretching from Belgium's North Sea coast 440 miles south through eastern France to the country's frontier with Switzerland. There, along what was being called the Western Front, the Germans faced off against the forces of the French and British and their allies.

Soon after Christmas, Norman and his platoon were transferred from Codford fifty miles north to Cheltenham, where they joined thousands of other soldiers in training. Once more, Norman was billeted in local housing while his men lived in huts. By now it was winter, and the training camp flooded with freezing rain, making everyone miserable. In these wretched winter conditions, the soldiers at Cheltenham began learning about the kind of trench warfare being used along the Western Front.

Senior officers described how in front of the trenches on the Western Front coils of barbed wire were strung out in long rows. The wire was intended to slow the advance of any German troops trying to attack across no-man's land, the barren, muddy strip between the German trenches and the Allied trenches. The fortified trenches of the Allies consisted of two lines of wide trenches from which soldiers kept watch on the enemy. The wide trenches were connected by narrower trenches, along which soldiers rotated in and out of the front lines. Behind the two lines of wide trenches were more trenches used for first aid, supply storage, and communication posts. Behind the trench system, members of the artillery had set up powerful guns that could fire massive shells across the trenches and deep into enemy lines. The soldiers at Cheltenham were soon learning how to dig trenches and tunnels and being trained in the logistics of living and fighting in them.

As he trained, Norman felt the need for closer Christian fellowship. He started a group called C.O., which stood for Christ's Own. The group started with a few of Norman's fellow officers who met to study the Bible and pray. Before long, thirty men were meeting together regularly. Norman's closest friend, Roger Fowke, who was the commanding officer, was part of the group, and Norman often asked him for advice on how to reach out to the troops and share the gospel with them.

Norman was aware that some of his early attempts to share the gospel with his men had come across as clumsy and off-putting. He once interrupted an illegal gambling game with the words, "I say, men, can I tell you something that is better than gambling, and that is to know Jesus Christ." No one seemed interested, but Norman kept talking anyway. He also spoke to the sergeant while they were route marching and to other officers while they were on parade, but with little success. And he often sat outside reading his Bible, hoping someone would see him and want to ask him questions.

Roger advised Norman not to create unnecessary barriers between him and the men. He suggested Norman take up smoking so he could talk to the other men as they sat around smoking. Norman followed this suggestion and started to smoke a pipe. He also carried a pack of cigarettes with him around training camp, stopping to share them with the enlisted men. He found they were much more ready to listen to his witnessing attempts as they smoked the cigarettes he offered.

In April 1915, after four months at Cheltenham, Norman, his platoon, and the rest of the battalion moved once more, this time to Sandhill Camp at Longbridge Deverill in Wiltshire, fifty miles south. Here the men received the long-promised rifles and bayonets, along with khaki uniforms. Although they were issued with cloth caps, it was rumored that steel helmets would soon be available. Norman was relieved to hear this. He couldn't imagine his men being involved in trench warfare with nothing but cloth to protect their heads.

On May 7, 1915, soon after arriving at Sandhill Camp, news came that a German U-boat had torpedoed and sunk the British passenger ship RMS *Lusitania* off the Irish coast. The ship had set sail from Liverpool and was on its way to New York in the United States when it was hit. The vessel sank in eighteen minutes, drowning 1,201 of the 1,900 passengers and crew aboard. The news was sobering for Norman. Soldiers were not the only ones being killed in war. Innocent civilians crossing the ocean on a passenger ship were also targets.

Now that they had real weapons, during the five months stationed at Sandhill Camp, Norman and his men practiced shooting their new rifles and ran through numerous bayonet drills until they were proficient. Norman and the other officers also took a keen interest in what was happening along the Western Front, where they believed they would soon be sent to fight. The truth was, not much had happened. There were attacks by both sides and massive artillery bombardment. The attacks, counterattacks, and bombardment inflicted severe casualties among the troops on both sides but produced no significant territorial advances along the Western Front, which remained in the same position it had for nearly a year.

On Tuesday, September 21, 1915, the moment twenty-year-old Second Lieutenant Norman Grubb had been awaiting arrived. His platoon took a troop train to Folkstone on the southeast coast of England and then boarded a naval transport ship bound for Boulogne-sur-Mer, France. Norman at last was on his way to fight in the war.

Chapter 5

Happy Valley

Upon arrival in Boulogne-sur-Mer, Norman and his platoon joined the 78th Brigade in the 26th Division of the Gloucestershire Regiment. After disembarking the troopship, they headed 135 miles south to Guignemicourt, where they were assigned to a stretch of the Western Front.

The thing Norman noticed most the first time he stepped into the trenches was the rats, which were everywhere. It was hard to even walk around in the trenches without stepping on one. Norman was soon introduced to an evening ritual. The men would sit with their guns at the ready, and when they saw the shadow of a rat running along the trench rim, they would aim and shoot. As dead rats rained down into the trench, Norman realized that some of the men were crack shots.

There also seemed to be an oversupply of tinned food on the Western Front, at least on the Allies' side, and Norman was surprised at how some of these extra rations were put to use. The sides of some of the trenches he was assigned to were built up to their twelve-foot height with stacks of hundreds of tins of bully beef.

As he walked around and adjusted to life in the trenches amid mud and rats, Norman every so often recognized a fellow Old Boy from Marlborough College. One night as he walked past a fellow officer, he turned to take a closer look at the man. To his surprise, it was Mayo McClenaghan, who'd been his study mate in their senior year at Marlborough. Norman was glad to see the familiar face, but his mood soon altered when Mayo told him his brother Bryant had already been killed in action, shot through the heart as he led a charge at Hooge. Norman had known Bryant well, and it saddened him to think that instead of taking up a scholarship in history at Cambridge, Bryant was now buried in foreign soil at the age of twenty.

Not long after learning of Bryant's death, Norman had his own brush with mortality. He and his men were digging a new trench about a hundred yards long. Norman was working at one end of the trench when a series of German five-inch shells, or clumps, as the men called them, rained down on the other end of the newly dug trench. Norman dove for cover as the acrid gunpowder smell from the incoming shells wafted along the trench. That was when something inside told him he should move from where he was taking cover to the place where the clumps had just fallen. Before he even thought about it, Norman was racing down the trench. As he reached the opposite end, he turned around just in time to see another burst of incoming clumps land right on the spot where he had taken cover. He knew he would have been dead and buried in France like Bryant McClenaghan if he hadn't reacted immediately to the voice within.

Norman had been in France seven weeks when a secret order arrived stating that he and his men were to pack up their gear and report for transport. Apparently the whole 26th Division was being moved, but no one knew where. Along with the rest of the 78th Brigade, Norman packed up and reported for transport in early November. He soon learned from a senior officer that they were being taken to the port of Marseilles in southern France and that orders as to where they were going would be unsealed once their troopship left port.

It was all a mystery as Norman and the rest of his brigade were crammed into cattle cars on the train for the trip south to Marseilles. Since no toilets were available in cattle cars, the train would stop regularly beside a field so the men could relieve themselves behind a tree or a bush. The stops were short. The train would sound its horn when it was about to leave, and on more than one occasion Norman laughed heartily as some of the men were forced to rush back to the train.

When the train reached Marseilles, the men transferred to a troopship, which Norman noted was
nearly as overcrowded as the train. As rumor had it,
once the ship had set sail it was announced they were
being transferred to Salonika. Norman scrambled to
find a map to see where that was. He stared at the dot
on the map marking Salonika's position. It was a city
in Greece situated at the head of the Gulf of Salonika
in the northwest corner of the Aegean Sea.

Norman and many of the others on the ship wondered, Why Salonika? The answer filtered down through
the officers. They were going to Salonika because the
month before, the Greeks had asked the Allied Powers
to aid their ally the Serbs, who were under attack from
Germany, Austria-Hungary, and Bulgaria.

As their ship sailed up the Gulf of Salonika, one of
the crew pointed out the spot, thirty-six miles south
of Salonika where three weeks before, another British
troopship, the SS *Marquette,* was torpedoed and sunk
by a German U-boat. The ship sank within ten minutes
of being hit, leaving hundreds of survivors struggling
in the water. One hundred sixty-seven men drowned
before rescue craft could reach them. It was a chilling
reminder to Norman of how dangerous travel by ship
could be with German U-boats marauding below. He
realized how blessed they had been on the journey
from Marseilles not to have been attacked.

After the troopship rounded a point and began
steaming northeast, the city of Salonika emerged over
the horizon. As they moved closer, Norman stood on
deck and peered at the city. From a distance the place

looked exotic, filled with white buildings and red tile roofs. Smoke rose from chimneys, and outdoor fires and minarets dotted the city skyline. After coming ashore, however, Norman discovered that looks could be deceiving. What seemed exotic at a distance was, as he stood amid it, smelly, noisy, dirty, and run-down. He was glad to be moved out of the city to the site where the men of the 78th Brigade would initially be housed—in bivouacs or lean-to style tents. It rained the whole time, and Norman soon learned they were camped in an area that flooded. Everything was soaked as water pooled in low spots or ran in torrents over the downhill incline of their camp. To make matters worse, when the rain stopped, snow began falling. There was no way to get warm in the bivouacs. Rations were limited, and Norman was hungry most of the time. Some of the other officers traded with the local people, who were unwelcoming and charged high prices for fresh produce and eggs.

Although the 78th Brigade had been brought to Salonika to aid the Serbs, by the time they arrived, the Serbs had been beaten. After days of waiting in bivouacs, military higher-ups decided the Bulgarian army situated to the north now posed a threat to Greece. To stop an invasion, newly arrived troops were to be stationed along the rugged, rocky mountains north of Salonika, where they would dig in and create a 250-mile-long barbed-wire fence. The hope was that the fence would stop the Bulgarians from advancing into Greece. The fence was soon dubbed the Birdcage because of all the barbed wire needed to construct it.

Norman and his platoon settled into their allotted space in the hills above the western tip of Lake Langaza, forty miles north of Salonika. They called it Happy Valley, but it was anything but happy. When they arrived the day after Christmas, the weather had turned brutally cold, and already three feet of snow lay on the ground as they set up their tents and established their camp. Despite the cold, Norman had to admit that the view from Happy Valley was stunning. Spread out in front of them on the plain below was Lake Langaza, its surface shimmering in winter sunlight.

Building the Birdcage turned out to be backbreaking work as they dug into rock with picks, hammers, and chisels. While they worked, Norman and his men kept an eye on the horizon, expecting the Bulgarian army to appear at any moment. It didn't, and the work on the Birdcage went on day after day, week after week along the hills. On occasion the men saw small German airplanes in the distance and learned they were dropping bombs on Salonika. Once or twice Norman even glimpsed a zeppelin floating toward the city. He later learned that in May the airship was shot down by guns from HMS *Agamemnon*, anchored in the bay at Salonika.

Life became monotonous for the men in his platoon. Norman did what he could to lift their spirits, as well as those of other members of the 78th Brigade. He held Bible studies in his tent and encouraged the men to talk openly with one another about their fears and frustrations.

As months dragged on, it became obvious that the Bulgarian army wasn't coming their way after all. All the digging and chiseling had been for nothing.

Just as the men were preparing to be relocated from their position on the hillside, a fierce summer storm whipped through camp. Norman awoke as his tent collapsed on top of him. He lay still for a moment, making sure he wasn't hurt. As he started climbing out from under the canvas, he wrenched his right knee, the same knee he had injured three years before playing rugby at Marlborough College. Excruciating pain shot up and down his leg as he struggled to get out from under the tent. By the time he'd crawled to safety on a rocky outcrop, he knew something was seriously wrong.

A medic examined Norman's knee and informed him he had again torn the cartilage in his knee. Once more, Norman would need surgery to repair it.

Norman was carried on a stretcher, first by hand and then by mule from Happy Valley and taken to a makeshift clinic at Lembet, where he was given a shot for the pain. He was then sent by truck to Salonika, where he was transferred to a ship bound for the island of Malta in the middle of the Mediterranean Sea, where the Allies had set up a hospital network. Most of the other men traveling on the ship with Norman were ill from malaria or dysentery. Not many of them were injured, as he was. In fact, an orderly aboard told him three times as many men were dying from various diseases than from battle wounds. Norman hoped he wouldn't catch something from them, crammed into the ship the way they were.

When Norman arrived on Malta, he learned that twenty-seven separate military hospitals were on the island that accommodated twenty-five thousand patients. Sick and wounded soldiers from Salonika and the Allied campaign at Gallipoli in Turkey were being brought to Malta for treatment at a rate of nearly two thousand men each week. Some of the hospitals were set up in solid buildings, such as schools, hotels, administrative offices, and old barracks, while others consisted of row upon row of canvas tents.

Since he needed surgery, Norman was taken to a hospital in a stone building that housed recovery wards as well as special X-ray apparatus and an operating theater. In late July 1916 Norman underwent surgery to repair the torn cartilage in his knee. He was still in the hospital ward recovering when he turned twenty-one on August 2. As he lay in his hospital bed, Norman wondered how his family was getting on and how his older brother Harold was faring in the fighting. Occasionally a letter would arrive from home keeping him up with the news, though usually by the time it got to him it was old news.

In October 1916, after spending nearly three months on Malta, Norman passed his medical examination and was pronounced fit to return to the war front. However, he was not sent back to his old brigade in Salonika. Instead he was drafted into the heart of the fighting on the Western Front in France, where he was to serve with the Fifth Battalion of the Gloucestershire Regiment.

Chapter 6

Where His Life's Work Lay

Norman joined his new battalion fighting along the Western Front in the Somme Valley of northeastern France. He had been fighting in the frontline trenches for eleven months when, on the moonlit night of September 21, 1917, the Allies made another attack on German lines. Norman and his platoon were part of the attack. He and his men took cover and awaited orders behind a pigsty about a mile from the attacking Allied line. Norman received word that things weren't going well for the Allied troops, who had managed to get caught up in German barbed-wire defenses as German machine gunners were mowing them down. He and his platoon were ordered to advance forward to capture Tombois Farm, a strategic piece of land held by the Germans.

Norman divided his platoon in two, with each group marching up one side of the road leading to the farm. As they moved along, several German shells exploded nearby. Norman was relieved that none landed on them. He was also relieved when the men reached the place where they expected barbed wire to be strung across the road and found the Germans had instead cut down two trees across the road to try to slow the advancing Allies. He and his men quickly scrambled over the trees and moved on. They were now behind the German lines as they headed down a sunken farm road, typical in the area.

Sloshing along the muddy road, Norman could see German dugouts in the steep bank, with defensive trenches along the top. Norman was nervous. Were the Germans still around? Were he and his platoon walking into an ambush? As the men pressed on, it at first appeared that the Germans had abandoned their fortifications. That was before Norman heard two soldiers speaking loudly in German behind them. He spun around and waited. When Norman felt their voices were close enough, he fired his rifle into the darkness. The conversation in German stopped abruptly.

As the platoon kept moving forward, they encountered a young German soldier kneeling next to and weeping over the body of a dead German officer. The members of his platoon called for Norman to shoot him. After all he'd been through, Norman felt like shooting the soldier, but something told him not to. Instead he ordered his men to take the German captive and send him back behind Allied lines as a prisoner of war.

Farther along the road in the waning moon-light, Norman and his men saw a group of Germans run across the road in front of them. The Germans seemed unaware that Allied soldiers were so close by. Norman supposed they were taken by surprise when hand grenades thrown by his men began exploding in their midst. By the time the sun came up, the German soldiers had fled and Tombois Farm was in the hands of Norman and his platoon. Follow-ing the capture of the farm, Norman learned he had been granted the Military Cross, an award given to officers for meritorious action.

A month after capturing Tombois Farm, Norman and his platoon were again in action. At quarter to four in the morning, Norman gathered his men and told them how risky their mission was. They were to advance a mile and capture a piece of strategic high ground in the face of a blistering German counter-attack. Knowing many of his men might not return alive from the mission, he encouraged them to accept Christ as their personal Savior. By four thirty it was as though the sky above them had burst into flames as hundreds of Allied artillery guns began bombard-ing German lines. For Norman and his men, it was zero hour—the offensive had begun. "Over the top!" he ordered and turned to climb one of the ladders leading to the top lip of the trench.

Norman surged forward with his platoon, rifles in front and bayonets attached, ready for whatever came their way. And what came their way was German machine-gun fire cutting horizontally across the battlefield. Norman saw soldiers around him collapse facedown in the mud. The rest kept advancing toward their target. They crossed a muddy stream and took shelter from bullets and mortar shells by crouching behind decimated fallen trees or jumping into shell craters from previous battles.

Norman took cover in a shell crater with a young private. There was another blast of machine-gun fire. Norman watched as the private slumped backward dead next to him. As Norman tried to assess the situation, he felt as though someone had hit him with a metal bar on the back of his right leg. He looked down. Blood oozed from a wound. He had been hit by a machine-gun bullet that entered just above his knee, passed through his thigh, and exited several inches higher up than it had entered. The advance on the Germans would go on, but without Norman. Using the rifle of the dead private as a crutch, he stumbled back toward Allied lines for treatment. A soldier headed out into the rain of machine-gun bullets and yelled, "Lucky Grubb! He's got a blighty!" At that moment Norman didn't feel so lucky. A blighty was a wound severe enough to take a soldier out of action but hopefully not serious enough to kill him.

After Norman made it safely to a first-aid dugout, a tight bandage was placed around his wound. Norman was lifted into an ambulance with several other men and taken from the battlefield to a makeshift military hospital behind the Western Front. From there,

Norman was put aboard a hospital ship for transport back to England.

Upon arrival in Folkestone on England's south coast, Norman was transferred to a hospital train and began a journey northwest toward London. As the train approached London, he assumed they would stop and the wounded would be taken to a hospital there. But the train didn't stop. It chugged through London and headed north through St. Albans, Luton, and Bedford before stopping at Leicester Station. An injured captain riding in the train suggested to Norman they might be headed for the old Leicester Lunatic Asylum, which had been converted into a military hospital for officers.

The captain was right. Norman and the other officers on the train were checked into one of the huge, rectangular red-brick buildings that had been hastily converted to house wounded soldiers. Each man was assigned a metal-frame bed with a kapok mattress and neatly folded sheets. Since he couldn't walk, two orderlies lifted Norman into bed. It was something he could only dream about sleeping on in the trenches in France.

Days passed slowly at the 5th Northern General Hospital, as the military hospital in the old asylum in Leicester was officially known. Everyone waited eagerly for new patients to arrive in hopes that they had up-to-date news of what was happening on the battlefront.

Norman already realized that even if the war dragged on, there was little chance he would be sent back to active duty. In just a year and a half he'd incurred two major injuries to his right knee, not to mention the original injury he had received while playing rugby at Marlborough College four years before. It seemed unlikely to Norman that he would be able to walk well on his injured knee for some time to come. This knowledge, along with hope that the war would soon be over, turned his thoughts toward what he should do next. He wanted to serve God, but how?

On the third day in 5th Northern General Hospital, a tall man about ten years older than Norman walked slowly through the ward. He stopped at each bed to talk with the wounded soldiers. Norman noted his clerical collar.

"Good afternoon, how are you? I'm Reverend Gilbert Barclay," the man said.

Norman pulled himself to a sitting position in bed. "Glad to meet you, Padre."

"Is there anything I can do for you or pray for you today?" Gilbert asked.

Norman sensed the man had a genuine faith, and soon the two of them were in deep conversation. Gilbert served as a chaplain to the wounded soldiers at 5th Northern General Hospital and was a Church of England clergyman and pastor of a church in Carlisle to the north. Norman eagerly told him how his father was a Church of England clergyman in Poole. As the two continued talking, Norman realized that one of his father's aunts lived in Carlisle. Gilbert informed him that he knew her well. She was an active member of his parish.

As Gilbert moved on to the next bed to talk to more wounded soldiers, Norman knew he'd made a friend.

A few days later, Gilbert returned to the hospital with his wife, Dorothy. She was beautiful, and Norman was impressed by the way her faith in Christ shone through. As they chatted, Norman learned that Dorothy had an unusual background. She was one of the four daughters of a man named Charles Thomas (C.T.) Studd. Since Norman hadn't heard of him, Dorothy explained that her father had been one of three famous cricketing brothers during the early 1880s in England. The Studd brothers' father, Dorothy's grandfather, made a fortune in India growing indigo, a flowering plant. Back in England he had attended a D.L. Moody evangelistic campaign meeting, where he became a Christian. His three sons, including C.T. Studd, soon followed their father in his newfound faith. Dorothy's father had attended Trinity College in Cambridge, where he was twice officially named best all-round cricket player in England. But when his older brother, George, became seriously ill, C.T.'s faith was stirred. Although England's top cricketer, he realized this was only a fleeting glory and that there was something far more important and glorious for a Christian—winning others to Christ.

In 1885, C.T. decided to become a missionary to China and joined China Inland Mission, founded by Hudson Taylor. Six other Cambridge students decided to follow Dorothy's father in the endeavor. They became known as the "Cambridge Seven," and all went to serve in China together. While there, C.T. met and married Priscilla Livingstone Stewart.

Dorothy explained to Norman that she and her three sisters were born in China, but after ten years, various health issues had forced the family to return to England. However, in 1900 the Studd family left England once more and this time headed to South India, where for six years C.T. served as pastor of a church in Ootacamund.

Once more, illness forced the family back to England. But to everyone's surprise, Dorothy explained to Norman with a glint in her eyes, her father had one more mission call to fulfill. Although over the age of fifty and suffering from asthma and tuberculosis, in 1913 C.T. set out for Africa. He settled in the northeast section of the Belgian Congo, which also happened to be the geographic center of the continent. He left with little financial backing and few prospects, leaving his wife and four grown daughters behind in England as he penetrated one of the least explored and evangelized places on earth.

Dorothy went on to say that her father, who would turn fifty-seven in a few days, was still in the heart of Africa proclaiming the gospel to the tribal people living among the forests. He had also started a mission to support the work he was doing, calling it The Heart of Africa Mission, or HAM for short.

Norman was intrigued by all Dorothy had told him about her father, and more so two days later when Gilbert returned to the hospital with a copy of a little magazine Dorothy's mother had put together. Norman read it with great interest, especially an excerpt from one of C.T. Studd's letters from the Congo:

May 14, 1917. The whole country round seems to be really greedy to hear the Word of God, many are deciding for Christ. We have 50 chief's sons in our school. Many chiefs are beginning to build schools and other houses at their centers, that we may go and instruct them and their people; everywhere we have an open door for ourselves and our native Christians; the Officials help us in every way. We are attacking the Ituri Province, and God has ordered that in a wonderful manner.

I brought my section of the party of seven by an unusual route, it led us through Pawa. We had not been three hours there before a Chief came and said he would give us a piece of land on which to settle and build and instruct his people, and if we could not come he and his retinue would come to Nala for six months to learn the Word of God! We decided to accept the offer, and sent some native Christians to see what ground was offered; the report was favorable. . . .

We had thirty baptisms just before A. [Albert] and E. [Edith] left here (May). . . . I sat opposite a crowd who desired baptism and were being instructed—the last meeting was being held. They were telling of their former lives and how they had learned of Christ and the power following their belief. It was strange to hear them quietly telling such stories as, "Formerly I was a very, very bad man, many men have I killed in my time." But then quite a youngster began to tell of his former bad deeds and said, "Many, very many men have I eaten, and my bad deeds were enormous and continuous."

Norman read the first sentence again: "The whole country round seems to be really greedy to hear the Word of God, many are deciding for Christ." As he read, he heard a clear voice inside his head say, "That's where you are to go." A shiver ran down Norman's spine. He was positive God had just directed him to join C.T. Studd and his mission in the heart of Africa. That was where his life's work lay.

Norman didn't waste any time. He wrote a letter to Dorothy's mother, Priscilla Studd, who lived in the mission headquarters in London, explaining how he felt called to join the Heart of Africa Mission. He included a donation with the letter.

By now Norman's knee was healing well. He could get around on crutches and dress himself, and before he received a reply from Priscilla to his letter, he was transferred from the 5th Northern General Hospital in Leicester to a convalescent home in Bournemouth, where he could be closer to his parents. A letter from Mrs. Studd arrived for Norman there. In the letter she invited him to come and stay with her anytime he was in London.

Two weeks after arriving at the convalescent home in Bournemouth, Norman ventured out on his own. He had an appointment with King George V at Buckingham Palace, where he was to receive the Military Cross he had earned for meritorious action in the taking of Tombois Farm in France. While in London he arranged to stay at the HAM headquarters. He was surprised to find the mission headquarters located in the grand old house on Highland Road in Upper Norwood, a suburb of southwest London, where Priscilla Studd lived. Norman was even more surprised to be greeted by a beautiful, dark-haired young woman who introduced herself as Miss Pauline Studd. He could see immediately she was the younger sister of Gilbert Barclay's wife, Dorothy. Mrs. Studd soon bustled over to welcome Norman. She was a big woman, with an even bigger smile, and Norman felt at home right away.

Norman loved everything about the fourteen-room Studd home at 17 Highland Road, but mostly he enjoyed talking with Pauline. He soon discovered she was an avid Bible scholar and a fearless witness for her faith. Norman also learned she was the youngest of the four Studd sisters. Grace, who had already been widowed, was the oldest. Dorothy was next, followed by Edith, who lived in Africa with her father and was about to marry Alfred Buxton, a fellow missionary. Then came Pauline, who lived with her mother in London. Pauline had a "war job" in London and traveled into the city by train each weekday.

On the day Norman was to receive his Military Cross from the king, Pauline helped him on and off the train as they traveled into London together. By the end of the trip, Norman was convinced he was in love with Pauline Studd and that they would one day marry.

Chapter 7

Brokenhearted

Back at the convalescent home in Bournemouth, Norman continued to recover from his injury. When he looked around at the injuries other soldiers were having to face—from blindness to amputated limbs—Norman was grateful that only his leg had been injured. By late summer 1918, Norman had recovered enough to be declared fit for active duty. But instead of going back to the Western Front in France, he was assigned the position of bombing officer in a training battalion based in Maidstone, Kent, about thirty miles from where Pauline Studd lived.

Like the other officers in the training battalion, Norman was billeted in a private home. Two homes were available to him, but when he discovered one of the homes belonged to a prominent Christian family, he asked to be billeted there. Frank Fremlin and his wife, Edith, lived in Warden House, one of the most beautiful houses in town, and Norman and Frank struck up a firm friendship.

The Great War in Europe continued to grind on. Back in early April 1917, the United States had been drawn into the fighting, and now ten thousand American soldiers were arriving in France each day to fight the Germans. People began to imagine that an end to the war might be in sight. With so many American soldiers in France, it would only be a matter of time before the Germans were worn down and beaten. Norman hoped so.

Sure enough, November 11, 1918, became a day Norman would never forget—Armistice Day. The Germans capitulated, and on that day at 11:00 a.m., "the eleventh hour of the eleventh day of the eleventh month," the Germans signed an armistice agreement with the Allies putting into effect an immediate ceasefire. The Great War was over!

Norman caught a train to London to be a part of the celebrations there. The streets of London were filled with people cheering and yelling and celebrating. Trafalgar Square was packed. And tens of thousands of people were gathered in front of Buckingham Palace. The noise in the streets was deafening. The entire city of London was caught up in an enormous spontaneous party.

The following day Norman asked Pauline to meet him in London so they could be part of the ongoing celebrations and have dinner together. After their meal, Norman and Pauline wandered through Trafalgar Square and along the Thames embankment. The celebrating crowds had thinned out as they reached Cleopatra's Needle and stopped beneath the monument. Much to his own surprise, Norman decided to ask Pauline to marry him. Terrified, he said, "Pauline, I love you, and I wonder if there's any chance that you would marry me."

"No, it can't be," he heard Pauline shoot back. Norman reeled from the rejection.

Pauline looked at him and then exclaimed, "Oh, no! I didn't mean that I won't marry you. I meant that it can't be that someone like you would want to marry me." She looked into Norman's eyes and then added, "Yes, I will."

That night Norman rode the train back to Upper Norwood with Pauline and spoke with Mrs. Studd, asking for her daughter's hand in marriage. On behalf of her and her husband, Mrs. Studd gave Norman her permission. It was settled. Pauline was to become Norman's wife. Norman was more excited by that than he was over the end of the Great War. His whole life was taking a wonderful turn.

Norman continued being billeted with the Fremlins while awaiting his decommissioning from the army. During that time, he learned that Cambridge University was offering education to servicemen who had been accepted by the university before the war but had put off attending so that they could join the military. If they undertook a course of study for one year and one term, four terms in all, at the university, they could earn a B.A. degree. Norman was tempted to sign up. He had been informed he would be released from military service in January 1919 and began praying about his future. One day, while Norman and Frank Fremlin were walking along the main street of Maidstone, Frank asked, "Are you thinking of taking up the offer at Cambridge?"

"Yes, sir," Norman replied. "It's on my mind."

"Well, if you believe God is directing you to go, I will pay for it," Frank said.

Norman was speechless. Suddenly the way seemed clear—he would go to Cambridge, get his degree in record time, marry Pauline, and then together they could head out to the Belgian Congo to start their missionary work. It was a great plan, although it didn't work out the way Norman had anticipated.

January 1919 was a time of new beginnings for many people in Europe. With the Great War over, it was time to get back to normal civilian life. As Norman arrived at Trinity College, Cambridge, he realized the university also bore the marks of four years of war. Only about ten percent of the student body was left, the rest having joined the war effort in some way, many of whom were now buried in graves on foreign soil. The university buildings had been used to house both Belgian refugees and officers of the hundreds of fighting platoons that trained on the sports fields. Across the River Cam, to the west of Trinity College in an area known as the Backs, a hospital had been hastily built on a cricket field shared by King's and Clare Colleges. The hospital, known as

First Eastern General Hospital, consisted of a series of prefabricated wooden huts and could hold seventeen hundred patients. From the beginning of the war in 1914, a constant stream of soldiers had been brought from the battlefront for treatment of injuries and wounds at First Eastern General Hospital. The entire town of Cambridge had been involved in helping run the hospital and care for patients. And now, as the hospital was being closed, everything and everyone in Cambridge, as in the rest of the country, was adjusting to a new "normal" where war and its effects were not the main focus of their lives.

Although studying at Trinity College, Norman didn't feel like a typical student. He was surrounded by ex-officers from colonels down to lieutenants who, like him, had decided to take advantage of the four-term degree. Many of them were still traumatized by their war experiences, and the professors didn't insist on strong test results.

Norman chose to study theology and geography but was soon disillusioned by his choice. He'd thought studying theology would equip him to be a better missionary. Instead he soon discovered that it meant endless debates on how Bible miracles could be explained away. Norman realized his mistake in looking for Christian fellowship and nurture in a theology class and asked to be allowed to study alone and take the test at the end of term. His tutor agreed, freeing Norman to spend more time with other young men who shared his evangelical faith.

Norman found a spiritual home with a group who pronounced their name "kick-you," which stood for Cambridge Intercollegiate Christian Union, or C.I.C.C.U. Pauline's father C.T. Studd, had attended Trinity College in the early 1880s before leaving for China as a missionary with six other Cambridge students in February 1885. The Christian students of Cambridge had built a chapel in town where they met each day to pray for their missionaries in China. It was named Henry Martyn Hall, after another graduate of Trinity College who had gone as an early missionary to India. The daily prayer meeting tradition in the hall continued, with Norman soon becoming a regular participant along with about ten other young men, including Murray Webb-Peploe and Godfrey Buxton. Godfrey was the younger brother of Pauline's brother-in-law, Alfred Buxton. Both of Godfrey's legs had been badly injured by shrapnel during the war, and he walked with the aid of two walking sticks. Each time the young men got together in Henry Martyn Hall, they prayed that God would open the hearts of other students so that they might come to know Christ. Within a short time, forty more students were joining the group regularly for prayer.

For Easter break in April 1919, Norman made his way down to London to spend a week with Pauline and her mother. On the train ride to London he began reading *Revivals of Religion* by Charles Finney. The book challenged and excited Norman. At the Studd house in Upper Norwood, Norman excitedly told Pauline about how Finney's book had shown him he would be missing out if he ever loved someone else more than God. Pauline sat with a flat, almost sad look on her face as he spoke.

The next day Pauline called Norman into the dining room. She took off her engagement ring, handed it to Norman, and told him she was breaking off the engagement. Norman was stunned, and no amount of pleading would make Pauline change her mind. She explained that he had become much too fanatical for her and that she didn't think she would be happy being his wife. Norman left London the next day to return to Cambridge brokenhearted. He had been certain that marrying Pauline was part of God's will for him. Now that didn't look like it was going to happen.

Back at Trinity College Norman burned the letters he'd received from Pauline and tried to get on with his life. But it wasn't easy. He missed Pauline deeply and wondered how things had gone so wrong when they had both felt it was so right to start with.

Norman also turned his attention to study. At the end of the term, he passed his exams, after which, at the start of summer vacation, he went to Highbury in North London to visit his Uncle George, where Norman told him about his breakup with Pauline. Uncle George was sorry the relationship hadn't worked out and then began talking about Norman's future. Norman listened patiently as his uncle explained why going to serve with the Heart of Africa Mission might not be the best for him now. George told his nephew the last thing he would want would be serving in

Africa with C.T. Studd, his almost father-in-law. And how would Norman feel if Pauline and the man she eventually married showed up on the mission field to serve alongside Norman? It would be a difficult situation for both of them. Uncle George suggested Norman instead consider going to India and serving with a small Indian mission he knew would gladly welcome Norman to work with them.

As Norman thought about his uncle's suggestion, he could see it had a certain logic. There was just one problem. As he prayed, Norman knew without a doubt that God had called him to work with C.T. Studd and his mission in the heart of Africa. While the mission position in India sounded attractive, Norman turned down Uncle George's suggestion.

In July Norman and several of his Cambridge friends set off for the northwest of England to attend the Christian convention held in the small town of Keswick. The Keswick Convention, which started in 1875, was held each summer, though it had been suspended during the war years. Now, in 1919, it was starting up again. Although Uncle George had been a speaker at the convention several times in the past and had told Norman all about the event, Norman was eager to experience it for himself.

The students from Cambridge, along with several students from Oxford University, twenty-eight in all, traveled north by train. One of the men traveling with them from Oxford was Noel Palmer, who at six feet, eight inches tall was nicknamed Tiny Palmer by everyone. Like Norman, Noel had been injured in the war, and the two became friends. And, like Norman, after healing from his wounds, Noel had gone off to study, only at Oxford instead of Cambridge.

Also traveling on the train was Pauline's mother. Priscilla had offered not only to rent two boarding houses in Keswick where the young men could stay but also to cook for all of them all during the convention. Norman had to admit it felt odd having the woman who could have been his mother-in-law traveling with them. Yet he was glad she was there. After all, she played an important role in the mission Norman felt called to join.

At first Norman was disappointed with his experience at Keswick. To him, the convention meetings seemed like so many church services he'd attended. He had expected a deeper experience. During the second week, five of the students, including Norman, decided to hold a prayer meeting one evening in a room at the boarding house. They intended for it to last a half hour, but none of the young men got up off their knees at the prayer meeting until 2:00 a.m., after praying together for hours on end. When Norman went to bed, he felt a joy he'd never experienced before. He also felt a closeness to his fellow students. After the prayer meeting, the second half of the convention was completely different for Norman from the first. Throughout the rest of the convention, he and his friends spent hours praying alone and in small groups.

A person Norman prayed for a lot at this time was his younger brother, nineteen-year-old Kenneth, who had recently declared himself an atheist. The declaration upset their father, who asked the rest of the family to pray for Kenneth. Norman prayed fervently for his brother's conversion and didn't stop until he felt certain that God had promised to answer his prayers and that Kenneth would become a Christian. With that, Norman wrote to his father informing him there was no more need to pray for Kenneth, that it was only a matter of time before he surrendered his life to Christ.

During the summer, Alfred and Edith Buxton and their one-year-old daughter, Susan, arrived back in England on furlough from serving with Edith's father, C.T. Studd, in the Belgian Congo. When Norman arrived back in Cambridge after his time in Keswick, he received a telegraph from Alfred asking him to meet him in London.

Norman traveled to London on the train, where he met Alfred and Edith face to face for the first time. A surprise was waiting for him. Alfred and Edith told him that Pauline was waiting for him. Norman raced to her. He didn't know how to act or what to say when he saw her again.

Pauline broke the ice. "When you came to stay last Easter and talked as you did, I said to myself, 'If I marry this man, I shan't even be second in his life. God will be first. God's work will be second, and I will be third. And I'll be third in no man's life.' So I broke off our engagement. But since then I've had time to reflect on my decision. Verse fifteen of Philemon spoke deeply to me at the time you asked me to marry you. In the verse Paul writes about Onesimus saying, 'Perhaps he therefore departed for a reason that thou shouldest receive him forever.' The verse recently came up again in my daily Bible reading. And with it, God nudged my heart. We are meant to be together!"

Pauline's words electrified Norman: his engagement to Pauline was back on. They would be husband and wife, after all.

Over the next several days, Norman had long conversations with Alfred and Edith. They spoke of life at Nala in the heart of Africa, the spiritual hunger of the people there, and how God had transformed people's lives through the power of the gospel. As Alfred retold some of the stories Norman had read in the HAM magazine while recovering in the hospital, the stories became even more alive in Norman's mind. And as the conversation continued, Norman's decision to serve as a missionary in the heart of Africa seemed more urgent than ever. He felt he needed to get to Africa sooner rather than later. Norman began considering giving up his studies at Cambridge at the end of the year and not finishing his degree so that he could go out and "help the old man spread the gospel message," as Alfred had put it.

In September 1919 Norman returned home to Bournemouth to visit his family. By now his young sister, Violet, was studying for a Bachelor of Science degree at Westfield College, a women's college at the University of London. His older brother, Harold, had returned home. He had served with distinction during the war as a signals officer and was awarded the Military Cross and Bar twice. Regrettably, Harold's heart was damaged during the war, and now he lived on a government pension. Norman's younger brother, Kenneth, was at home too, and their mother doted over her three sons.

On his second night at Bournemouth, Norman decided to attend what everyone agreed was a dull weekly prayer meeting at the church, attended mostly by old women. To his surprise, Kenneth asked to go with him. Norman tried to discourage him. If anything would confirm Kenneth's view that Christianity was old-fashioned and irrelevant to today's youth, it would be a group of old women praying. However, Kenneth insisted on going, so the brothers set out together. During the prayer meeting Norman prayed aloud, while Kenneth didn't utter a word. *Why would he?* Norman asked himself. *Kenneth, after all, claims to be an atheist.*

The next morning Kenneth bounded into Norman's bedroom and sat down on his bed. He told Norman that God had spoken to him during the prayer meeting the night before and that he'd hardly slept all night wrestling with the idea of being a Christian. He said he felt God say to him that if he did change his mind and become a Christian, He wanted the say over the whole of him, not just parts of him. Kenneth looked into Norman's eyes and told him that that was what he had done. He had given himself one hundred percent to God and swept aside his infatuation with atheism.

Norman was delighted and somewhat amazed at how swiftly God had answered the prayers he'd prayed in Keswick. God was alive, He answered prayer, and He was firmly leading the next chapter of his life. Of that Norman was certain.

Chapter 8

More Stubborn Than He'd Ever Imagined

Norman returned to Cambridge for what he now knew was his last term of study. He'd committed to depart for Africa at the end of December 1919 and would not return to university the next year for the final term to earn his degree. Since he was no longer looking to earn a degree, Norman set himself the task of personally inviting each student at Trinity College, all nine hundred of them, to C.I.C.C.U. gatherings and, if possible, speaking to them about Jesus Christ and the gospel. While it was a noble goal, Norman dreaded knocking on doors and introducing himself. He had no idea how each student would respond. And although he was secretary of C.I.C.C.U., he still felt nervous speaking about his faith without an invitation. Nonetheless, Norman prayed that God would embolden him, and he began knocking on the doors of fellow students. Many of the rooms he visited were inhabited by students who, like him, had served in the war and had then taken up Cambridge University's offer of a four-term Bachelor of Arts degree. Norman had a natural affinity with these students that allowed him to speak boldly about his faith, and he was surprised by the results. At least sixteen young men responded to what he said and committed their lives to Christ.

Other members of the C.I.C.C.U. were also surprised by the results. New members began attending their meetings, and old members asked Norman to tell them more about his approach, which he was happy to do. As he spoke with them, he felt a voice inside him say, "Shouldn't every university and college in Great Britain, and then in the world, have some kind of union of Christian students like the C.I.C.C.U.?"

As Norman pondered the voice he had heard, he wondered if it was possible, before he left for Africa, to arrange an event where members of C.I.C.C.U. and Christian students from other universities could get together to talk and fellowship. He talked to two of his friends, Clarence Foster and Leslie Sutton, about the idea. Norman wondered aloud if there was enough time before his departure for the Belgian Congo to secure a hall in London and ask Christian students from Oxford, London, and Durham Universities to come and meet with fellow Christian students from Cambridge in a first ever InterVarsity Conference. Clarence and Leslie agreed to look into the matter.

The day Norman once thought would never happen arrived at last. On Monday, November 24, 1919, Norman and Pauline were married in Upper Norwood. To save money on their wedding, they decided to forego a traditional wedding dress and formal suit. Norman stood tall in his only suit, and Pauline wore a blue travel dress. Norman couldn't have been happier. Noel Palmer was his best man, and Gilbert Barclay, Pauline's brother-in-law and the man who introduced him to the Heart of Africa Mission, officiated the wedding. Gilbert's wedding sermon was based upon Ecclesiastes 4:9–12: "Two are better than one . . . and a threefold cord is not easily broken."

Priscilla Studd and Alfred and Edith Buxton (Edith pregnant with her second child) were in attendance, as were Norman's three siblings, older brother, Harold; sister, Violet; and younger brother, Kenneth.

When Norman was discharged from the army, the government had given him nine hundred pounds, an amount calculated according to his rank and length of service. Following their wedding, Norman and Pauline had decided to spend this money on preparations for their missionary endeavor after they were married. And they had decided that when the money ran out, they would "live on faith," as so many others in the mission field had done before them. However, their living on faith was forestalled when Frank Fremlin offered to pay all of their expenses to get to the Congo.

In early December 1919, the first ever InterVarsity Conference (IVC) was held in London. About sixty

Christian students from various universities and colleges attended the event. It was so successful that at the end of the conference, they all agreed to make it an annual event. Norman had felt God call him to start the conference, and now that he was about to leave Great Britain, he was delighted that it would continue on without him.

On Wednesday, December 24, 1919, Christmas Eve, Norman and Pauline stood side by side by on the deck of an ocean liner as they sailed away from England. Next to them stood Lilian Dennis, a nurse also on her way to the Congo to serve with the mission. Norman looked forward to relaxing for the next several days as the ship made its way to Alexandria, Egypt. It had been a whirlwind year for him. For a while he'd thought all was lost, but now here he was, married to Pauline for a month and on his way with her to serve God in the heart of Africa. He looked at the new wristwatch some of the men from C.I.C.C.U. gave him as a going-away present. "Hallelujah" was inscribed on the back, and he knew that every time he looked at the watch, it would remind him of the Christian fellowship he enjoyed while at Cambridge.

Pauline's mother had been a great help in guiding the couple to the right things to take to the mission field. Packed away in traveling trunks in the ship's hold were two canvas camp beds, mosquito nets, a canvas camp table and chair, enamel plates and cups, and sturdy cooking pots. Priscilla had also advised them on basic clothing to take along. When Norman reached Africa, his daily attire would be much like his army uniform—khaki shorts and shirts, long socks and boots, with the addition of a pith helmet. Tucked inside their trunks were some specialty food items—cans of potted meat and Nestle's condensed milk, as well as some medicines for C.T. Studd.

As they sailed away, Norman tried to imagine how excited C.T. would be to have his daughter and son-in-law working alongside him. At the prayer meeting before the ship sailed, the mission's executive committee chairman told Norman, Pauline, and Lillian that they were charged with bringing help, refreshment, and encouragement to the tired band of missionaries holding on in the jungle. Norman prayed that he would be up to the task.

The voyage took eleven days, with the ship docking in Alexandria on Sunday, January 4, 1920. After disembarking, Norman sent a telegram to Priscilla in London informing her they had all arrived safely in Alexandria and were about to embark on the next leg of their journey. From Alexandria, the three of them caught the train south and then transferred to a riverboat that took them up the Nile River to Khartoum in Sudan.

In Khartoum they boarded a flat-bottomed stern-wheel paddle steamer for the thousand-mile trip along the White Nile River to Rejaf. For the first two hundred miles south of Khartoum, the land on either side of the river was flat and dry, much like the territory they had passed through in Egypt. The land was inhabited by Baggara Arabs, who tended herds of sheep, goats, cattle, donkeys, horses, and camels. The Baggara men wore white cotton tunics, while the women covered themselves head to foot in dark-blue cotton dresses. They all lived in flat-roof mud huts clustered along the river. As the steamer moved farther south, the arid landscape began to give way to forests.

Norman noticed that the huts the people lived in were different. The roofs were no longer flat but were conical and thatched. Also, the people who inhabited this area intrigued Norman. They were tall, slender people who liked to stand straight on one leg while resting the opposite foot against the knee of the supporting leg. They were completely naked except for the spear each man carried. "Those are Dinkas," one of the crewmen told Norman. "They live on the east bank of the river, and the Shillooks live on the western side."

Norman noticed somethings else as they made their way up the river. Crocodiles and hippopotami were everywhere, and their beady eyes could be seen above the waterline.

At night the paddle steamer stopped along the riverbank so that more wood could be loaded aboard to fire the boiler. The farther upstream the steamer went, the narrower the river became. Two weeks after setting out from Khartoum, they reached Rejaf in the south of Sudan. Beyond Rejaf the river was turbulent and ran through rapids that riverboats could not negotiate. It was now time to leave the Nile and river steamers behind and set out overland.

In Rejaf, Norman and Pauline paused to remember A.J. Bowers, who died there five years before from a tropical fever on his way into the heart of Africa to join C.T. Studd. Afterward, they climbed into a truck that would take the three missionaries a hundred miles southwest to the Belgian Congo border.

When they arrived at the border, several HAM missionaries were there to greet them. Norman breathed a sigh of relief when he learned that C.T., or "Bwana," as everyone called him, was still in good health. The missionaries who greeted them had hired everything necessary for the three-hundred-mile overland journey to Nala. Porters carried the luggage, and the women in hammocks strung between them, while the men walked or rode bicycles where they could. As they trudged through grasslands day after day, Norman could hear the rustle of animals moving in the long grass around them. When the grassland at last gave way to trees, they knew they had reached the Congo rain forest. From there the journey became slower as they were forced to follow narrow tracks through the dense forest towering above them.

After nearly two weeks of trekking overland, one of the guides informed Norman that they were nearing Nala. Sure enough, two hours later, the narrow trail they had been following opened to become a well-defined road lined with majestic palm trees. The road led right into Nala. The scene was exactly as Norman had imagined it. Nala had once been a Belgian outpost and so consisted of defined streets lined with solid brick buildings, remnants of its Belgian occupation, interspersed with traditional mud huts with thatched roofs. Nala also had a church and a school building. As the group approached Nala, schoolchildren and people from the village ran to meet them and escort them to the center of town, where Pauline was reunited with her father and Norman met his father-in-law for the first time. C.T. was tall and gaunt and sported a bushy beard, and he welcomed Norman enthusiastically.

The locals soon took to calling Norman Pa Rubi, apparently the best native approximation of Grubb. Several days after arriving, Norman wrote in a letter to the folks in England, "Well it is good, good, good to be here and to meet C.T. He's not well I'm afraid, so tired, but there's no stopping him."

Within weeks of arriving in Nala, Norman and Pauline realized they had misunderstood what working with C.T. Studd would be like. They'd expected a warm welcome, followed by an equally warm working relationship. Norman had imagined his father-in-law handing off some of the administrative work to him and gradually letting him take a leadership role. But none of that happened. C.T. carried on as if they were not even there. Pauline was also upset by the way her father treated her no differently from any of the other women in the mission. C.T. suffered from stomach problems, and when Norman urged him to let Pauline organize his meals, he rejected the idea, saying, "As long as we missionaries travel first class, live out of tins, eat bread and butter, and drink tea, the world will never be evangelized!" It seemed to Norman that C.T. was more stubborn than he'd ever imagined a fellow human being could be.

Despite C.T.'s poor health, Norman soon realized that he could not outwork his fifty-nine-year-old father-in-law. C.T. rose each morning at four o'clock to pray. He also played rousing songs on his banjo to attract local Christians to arise and pray with him.

As time went on, Norman and Pauline struggled to find where they fit into the mission. No one seemed to need the encouragement they wanted to offer. No one was flagging. It was quite the opposite. The people welcomed Norman, Pauline, and Lillian to Nala as though they were extra soldiers arriving on a long and active war front.

Nonetheless, like his own father, Norman discovered he had an aptitude for learning a language, even though he had never applied himself to learning Latin at school. But in the heart of Africa, things were different. Two hundred fifteen different languages were spoken in the Belgian Congo, though the most common language was Bangala, which the people used for trade. As a result, C.T. insisted that HAM missionaries first learn to speak Bangala instead of any of the other local dialects. Norman's brother-in-law, Alfred Buxton, had already compiled a simple Bangala/English dictionary and translated the Gospel of Mark into the language. With the help of Alfred's dictionary, it didn't take long for Norman to learn Bangala. Soon he was proficient enough in the language to preach at Sunday meetings.

Once Norman had learned the basics of the Bangala language, C.T. assigned him and Pauline to the newly established mission outstation at Deti Hill, twenty-five miles, or a two-day journey from Nala. Although the place currently had no "full-time" missionary, four hundred people met regularly for Christian fellowship and instruction.

Upon arrival at Deti Hill, Norman was relieved to see that a round bamboo hut had been built for them. The place was sturdy, and from its hillside location, it had a commanding view across the vast sea of tropical forest surrounding them. It would also be a comfortable new home for Pauline, who was expecting a baby around Christmas.

As they settled in at Deti Hill, Norman felt he had a better idea about how to run a more efficient mission station than the one in Nala. He set to work making Deti Hill a model for other missionaries to follow. Most Africans liked to acquire articles of Western clothing, which they prized and wore to church meetings and other Christian gatherings. But Norman felt this was wrong, that African Christians should wear African clothing when they went to church, and especially when they shared the gospel in surrounding villages. While the local Christians resisted Norman's new rule about not wearing Western clothing, Norman insisted they follow it strictly.

Within months of instituting the new rule, the numbers of locals attending mission meetings dwindled from four hundred to eighty. Norman prayed, asking God what had gone wrong. One word came to his mind—*pride*. Norman felt God speak to him, and he realized he had judged many of the things C.T. had done without ever grasping the method in his planning. This revelation caused Norman to write to his father-in-law, confessing his pride and asking to return to Nala, where he could learn how to be an effective missionary in the Belgian Congo. C.T. wrote back to Norman and Pauline, inviting them to return to and live in Nala.

Soon after the Grubbs settled back into life at the mission station in Nala, Alfred and Edith arrived. They had decided to leave their two children, Susan and newborn son, Lionel, with Alfred's parents in England and were missing them terribly. Alfred and Edith had lots of news to pass along. The executive committee in England had given the Heart of Africa Mission a new name. Going forward, HAM was to be known as the Worldwide Evangelistic Crusade, or WEC. Using the new name would allow the mission to branch out and begin evangelizing in other areas of the world. In keeping with that goal, Alfred reported that shortly before his departure for Africa, he and Priscilla Studd had visited the United States, where they raised funds for the work in the Belgian Congo and recruited Americans to train as WEC missionaries.

It all sounded very exciting to Norman as he and Pauline prepared for the birth of their baby. On December 2, 1920, everyone at Nala celebrated C.T.'s sixtieth birthday with a cup of tea and soda bread. As he sipped his tea, Norman took a long look at his father-in-law. C.T.'s hair was rapidly graying, many of his teeth had cracked or broken, and his dark, leathery skin and sunken eyes made him look decades older. Living in the rain forest had taken a toll on C.T.'s body.

Seventeen days later, on December 19, Noel Studd Grubb made his appearance into the world. He was the second white baby born in the heart of the Belgian Congo, the first being Edith Buxton's daughter, Susan. Everyone in the village celebrated Noel's arrival with Norman and Pauline.

With his grandson safely delivered, C.T. announced that he was about to leave Nala. In his opinion, the missionary work there was settled and he was called to pioneer new fields. He set his sights on establishing a new mission base in Ibambi, forty miles to the south.

In Nala, after C.T.'s departure for Ibambi, life fell into a new routine for the Grubb family. Norman made many treks into the forest to visit remote groups of Christian converts and hold evangelical meetings, while Pauline stayed close to Nala with the new baby. However, about the time Noel began teething, he became sick with bronchitis and stopped putting on weight. Everyone was concerned for his condition and offered Norman and Pauline help and advice. Slowly Noel began to get stronger, and Norman was convinced his son would return to full health.

On Noel's first birthday, December 19, 1921, Norman was visiting a Christian chief named Mofoi when a runner arrived from Nala with bad news— Noel had died. Knowing he needed to get back to Pauline as soon as he could, Norman organized a group of local men to accompany him. The men all carried spears to ward off dangerous animals as they traveled through the thick jungle in the middle of the night. The journey was scary, but Norman wanted to get to Pauline as quickly as possible. They'd both believed their son was gaining strength, and now he was gone.

Norman and his entourage arrived in Nala at eleven o'clock the next morning. Noel's little body lay in a simple wooden box lined with white embroidered fabric. Pauline had placed a pink daisy in his hands. By four o'clock the men of the village had cleared a shaded spot under some palm trees, where a funeral service was held. They sang "Jesus Loves Me," and Alfred Buxton said a few words before Noel's coffin was buried. Noel was the first white baby to die in the northwestern Belgian Congo.

Norman had little time to mourn the death of his son. Following Noel's burial, Pauline became seriously ill with anemia. Not wanting to take any risks with his wife's health, Norman insisted she be taken to Aba, two hundred miles to the northeast. The African Inland Mission in Aba had a hospital staffed by Western doctors who could treat Pauline. Norman organized a traveling party, and they set out for Aba. Pauline was carried in a hammock that hung from a sturdy pole held at each end by a porter. Norman walked by her side as they tried to cover the distance as fast as they could.

Norman was grateful that Pauline survived the trip and that a veteran Baptist missionary doctor, Dr. Roy Woodhams, was there to meet them upon arrival. Dr. Woodhams examined Pauline, and with a grim look on his face he explained to Norman that he thought she had pernicious anemia, for which there was no cure. He assured Norman he would treat her for regular anemia in case he'd made the wrong diagnosis. Pauline was admitted to the hospital and given medications and a special diet.

Much to the doctor's amazement, Pauline responded to the treatment. Norman was elated. The loss of Noel had been such a blow that he could hardly imagine what it would be like to lose his wife as well.

Pauline continued to improve, and since she needed a lot of rest as part of her recovery, Norman found himself with a lot of spare time. He decided to try his hand at translation work. He looked in the hospital library for a suitable project to start on and found a simplified version of *Pilgrim's Progress*, which he began translating into Bangala. The work went smoothly, and Norman enjoyed the challenge.

Meanwhile, Pauline's health steadily improved, causing Dr. Woodhams to pronounce that it was not pernicious anemia after all, but was the regular anemia which, if treated, was not fatal.

In February 1922, six weeks after arriving at the hospital in Aba, Pauline was well enough to return to Nala. Upon their arrival, Norman and Pauline received a joyous welcome from the missionaries and local Christians.

Two months after arriving back at Nala, Norman and Pauline set out with three newly arrived missionaries, the Kirks, an American couple, and a single woman, for Poko, a district of about 125,000 people sixty miles west of Nala. Other missionaries had worked there, and small groups of converts were scattered throughout the area. The plan was to use the village of Poko as a headquarters, but most of the time, the missionaries would be trekking through the Ituri Forest, challenging those who had not yet heard the gospel and encouraging those who were trying to live Christian lives under very difficult conditions. Of the work they were doing, Norman wrote,

> There is nothing like a mass movement here towards the gospel, but nearly everywhere there are little groups whose hearts the Lord has opened . . . about 30 centers of light scattered through this huge district, where there are groups of believers varying from 10 to 100. These cannot read the Word and live in the midst of unspeakable sin and temptation, so we have a big responsibility to be faithful shepherds to them, and for this we have a band of about 20 native evangelists who can mostly read and know the fundamentals of the gospel. But we have hardly touched our district yet, and there are numberless open doors as soon as we can enter. I know at this moment of six or seven chiefs who want us to come and preach to their people.

The letter was reprinted in a twice-yearly compilation of letters and circulated to a group of like-minded students from Cambridge University calling themselves the Cambridge University Missionary Band, or C.U.M.B. Norman became an active participant in the group, writing newsy, interesting letters about his missionary work as often as he could.

News from Great Britain was heartening. Three new missionary recruits, Jack Harrison, Jack Scholes, and George Kerrigan, were training for service in the Belgian Congo. All three men had recently been discharged from the army and were expected to arrive in July 1922. With more workers on their way to serve in the mission, Norman and Pauline began to plan a trip home to England.

Chapter 9

Watch Out for God

In June 1923, Norman and Pauline stood on the deck of their ocean liner carrying them home as they watched the coastline of England come into view. They had left England for the Belgian Congo three and a half years before, though in many ways it seemed a lifetime ago to twenty-seven-year-old Norman. He and Pauline went out as wide-eyed newlyweds and were returning with a wealth of experience beyond their years, including the birth and death of their only child. Norman could now clearly see he'd gone to work with C.T. Studd with his mind filled with idealistic views of missionary life. He understood that you take your problems with you: if you struggled with something in England, you would most likely struggle with it on the mission field.

The England Norman and Pauline returned to was far different from the place they had left. Many more motorcars than horse-drawn carts were now on the roads, and young people danced away the memories of the Great War to jazz music. Young women wore their hair and dresses shorter, and some smoked and drank in public, even driving motorcars. It was a long way from what they'd experienced in the heart of Africa.

Back at mission headquarters in Upper Norwood, Norman and Pauline were received warmly. They were also on a list of towns and cities throughout Great Britain wanting a WEC missionary to come and speak. Before long the Grubbs were touring the country speaking at churches and in village halls. They were also able to say farewell to Norman Lang, the fourth missionary WEC was sending to serve on the new mission field it had opened in South America. Norman was delighted to pray for Norman Lang, and as he prayed, he recalled the words of his father-in-law when he had set out for the Congo. "This journey is not just for Africa, but for the whole unevangelized world." Now, on the tenth anniversary of the founding of the mission, these words were coming true. Gilbert Barclay told Norman of the mission's plans to expand into Central Asia and Arabia. In fact, three pioneer WEC missionaries had recently set out to establish mission bases in Arabia, Afghanistan, and French Sudan. At the same time, Norman's younger brother, Kenneth, left on a tour of European libraries to research what was known about the tribal groups and the languages they spoke in the Amazon Basin. The plan was for Kenneth to go to South America later in the year armed with all the information he'd gleaned in Europe and pave the way for many more WEC missionaries to serve there.

Norman and Pauline had expected to stay in England for only six months before returning to the Belgian Congo, but Gilbert had confided in Norman that he was exhausted from his work as home director for WEC and needed a long break. Having agreed to take over the position while Gilbert rested, Norman put off plans to return to the Congo. On March 9, 1924, after they'd been home for nearly a year, Pauline gave birth to another baby boy. They named him Paul, and Norman watched anxiously for signs of poor health. He needn't have been concerned. Paul thrived right from the beginning.

Norman discovered that his temporary position required a lot of travel, including a visit to the United States to help the first group of American missionary recruits preparing to serve with WEC.

Along with keeping up with his busy travel schedule, Norman took on Gilbert's job editing the WEC magazine. Although he wasn't sure he was up to the task, he enjoyed it and tried to write in a lively manner, avoiding clichés and making sure all facts were double-checked for accuracy. Before long Norman found himself contemplating the power of the written word to inspire Christians to become missionaries.

In early 1925, the mission received news that Fenton Hall, a member of the first batch of WEC missionaries in the Amazon Basin, had died. Before joining WEC, Fenton, a former heavyweight boxer, had been an officer in the Royal Air Force. He died on Christmas Day of fever and dysentery, seven months after arriving in Amazonia. Two months later, a trunk containing Fenton's belongings arrived at WEC headquarters in London. Among the items in the trunk was Fenton's journal. Norman picked it up and began to read, and what he read amazed him. There and then Norman knew he should edit the journal and publish it so that others might be challenged to continue Fenton's work.

In June 1925, Gilbert resumed his responsibilities as WEC home director. Two years had passed since Norman and Pauline had returned from Africa to England for a six-month furlough. It was time to return to the Belgian Congo. By now Pauline had given birth to another baby, a daughter, born on April 8, 1925, who was named Priscilla, after her grandmother. As they contemplated returning to the Congo, Norman decided he should go alone, leaving Pauline and the two children in England. Neither he nor Pauline thought it was a good idea for young children to live in the disease-ridden forests of the Congo. Rather than leave their children at home with his parents, Pauline and Norman agreed they should be the ones to bear the burden of separating the family. Norman would go alone, expecting to be gone five years.

By the time Norman returned to the Congo, WEC was in turmoil—or at least the mission's executive committee in England thought so. The seven Americans who had recently arrived as WEC missionaries

Watch Out for God

to the Congo were mostly Baptists, while the British missionaries tended to be from Church of England or Methodist backgrounds. With the arrival of the Americans, a vigorous debate had arisen between them and their British counterparts over the meaning of certain Bible verses. Instead of trying to keep the two groups working harmoniously for the good of evangelizing the Congolese, C.T. Studd had waded into the debate and sided firmly with the British missionaries. Within weeks the Americans all resigned from WEC in the Belgian Congo and joined the African Inland Mission (AIM). This turn of events had caused an uproar, and it was especially hard for Norman, who'd been to the United States and personally helped the American missionaries prepare for their new life in Africa. When Norman got back to the Congo, C.T. was adamant that if God had really called the American missionaries to work with WEC, they would have stayed with the mission regardless of the conflict. Norman was left wondering whether WEC could ever be an international organization that worked across denominations.

Despite the situation with the American missionaries, C.T.'s work at Ibambi was going well. Yet the executive committee was concerned that in addition to arguing with the Americans, C.T. was not doing enough to open new mission fields in other countries. The committee made it clear to Norman that he was to tell his father-in-law it was time for him to come home and take a role in the mission's international leadership under their guidance. C.T. strongly disagreed. He

believed that WEC would one day have missionaries
in many countries, but that it was not his job to make
that happen. Each missionary had to find their own
call and financial support, and WEC would function
as the umbrella organization that sent them out.

Soon after Norman's arrival, C.T. received a letter
from Alfred Buxton. In it Alfred explained that he and
Edith were in the United States trying to smooth over
issues regarding the American missionaries who'd
been sent to the Congo. By the time C.T. had finished
reading the letter, his face was red with anger. C.T.
considered Alfred's being in the United States doing
what he was doing an act of disloyalty. Immediately
he sent off a reply dismissing Alfred and Edith from
the mission. Norman was stunned. Not only was
Alfred the man who'd accompanied C.T. into the
heart of Africa thirteen years before when no one else
would, but also he was the man's son-in-law. It took
every ounce of Norman's self-control not to resign on
the spot and leave C.T. to his own resources.

At Ibambi, Norman received a letter from Pauline
informing him that his father had died on September
12, 1925, at the age of 77. As he grieved his father's
death, Norman wrote to his mother offering his sympathy, love, and support as she moved on alone.

Meanwhile, letters and accusations had begun
to fly back and forth between C.T. and the executive
committee. After a year, C.T. asked Norman to return
to England and explain his position to the committee
once and for all, that is, that C.T. planned to stay in
the Belgian Congo until he died and had no intention
of returning to England to work in an office.

Norman wasn't confident he could change the minds of the executive committee members, but he dutifully returned home, arriving back in England in December 1925, having been gone for just six months. He got back just in time for Kenneth's return from Amazonia, where he'd started compiling an accurate and up-to-date map of the known tribes in the area and their languages. Soon afterward, Norman and Pauline attended Kenneth's marriage to Eileen, a woman he had known since they had lived near each other in Oxton. Another family event also took place. Norman's sister, Violet, earned her Ph.D. in science from London University and soon afterward left for China to become a schoolteacher with the Church Missionary Society.

As instructed by his father-in-law, Norman met with the members of the mission's executive committee. He knew and respected the men who formed the committee and hoped he could settle the issue they had with C.T.'s refusal to return to England to take an active role in the international leadership of WEC. He patiently explained to them that C.T. had no intention of returning to England and how C.T. felt it wasn't his job to open up new mission fields when God had clearly called him to labor in the Belgian Congo. But while the members of the executive committee conceded the point, Norman doubted the mission had heard the last of it regarding the issue.

While back in England, Norman was able to work on a new project he had embarked upon—translating the New Testament in the Bangala language. It was a daunting task, but Norman kept at it.

In April 1926, after spending just four months at home, Norman once more said goodbye to Pauline and returned to the Congo, where he intended to spend the next five years. Back in Ibambi, Norman gave his father-in-law a report of his meeting with the mission's executive committee in London. While C.T. had no intention of ever returning to England, Norman could see that he was giving a lot of time to contemplating the future of the mission. C.T. ultimately decided that the place for Norman and Pauline was in Great Britain, where they could assume the leadership of WEC upon C.T.'s death. Norman argued that he had been called to the Belgian Congo, not England. However, his father-in-law was adamant, and after a year with C.T. at Ibambi, Norman returned home, arriving in London in May 1927.

Once home, Norman explained to the executive committee that C.T. Studd had sent him home for good, and why. He could immediately see that this made several members of the committee deeply suspicious of C.T. and his motives. Nonetheless, Norman threw himself into the work of helping manage and grow the mission. As part of this, he set out on a mission deputation tour of Canada in December 1927.

For the next several months, Norman crisscrossed Canada, preaching at churches and speaking about the many WEC mission opportunities around the world. As he traveled, he had to admit that he'd never been so cold in all his life. It was winter in Canada. Everywhere he went, snow lay on the ground and howling winds sometimes dropped the temperature to minus 20 degrees Fahrenheit. At times it felt to Norman as though his hands and feet were frozen solid. But the warm reception he received at the churches he visited made it all worthwhile.

As he traveled, he also looked out for InterVarsity Christian unions where he could speak. To his surprise, he found that nothing like C.I.C.C.U. existed in Canada. He made a note to talk with Clarence Foster and the InterVarsity committee back in England about sending a representative to both Canada and the United States to get InterVarsity Christian groups established.

In late March 1928, after nearly four months of traveling and speaking around Canada, Norman returned to London. He arrived just in time for the birth of his and Pauline's fourth child, a son born on April 1, 1928. They named him Daniel.

That summer, around the time Norman turned thirty-three on August 2, the Grubb family, along with Priscilla Studd and others staying at WEC headquarters in London, headed north to Keswick for the annual Christian convention. Norman always looked forward to Keswick for spiritual refreshment and fellowship, and this year's convention was even more special when about halfway through, he was visited by a man introducing himself as Rees Howells. Norman recognized the name, remembering that at some point Rees had been a missionary in South Africa. Rees was sixteen years older than Norman, a solid man with a strikingly large forehead, protruding ears, and enormous hands, the right one with which he vigorously shook Norman's hand. After the introduction, the two men talked about what they were learning at Keswick. Rees also invited Norman to visit him at the new Bible college he'd set up in Wales. Thinking it rude to say no, Norman halfheartedly agreed to visit the college in the fall.

At the end of the Keswick convention, Norman returned to work at WEC headquarters. Within the mission, things were getting more difficult each day. By the end of September 1928, Norman was ready for a break and decided to visit Rees at his home in the beautiful Welsh countryside. Upon arriving, Norman sat down to talk with Rees. He soon realized he had seriously underestimated Rees's spiritual insight. For the first time in a long time, Norman was able to unburden his soul to someone. He told Rees how Alfred and Edith Buxton had been forced from the mission and how a part of him wanted to join Alfred in starting a new, less drama-filled mission in Africa. He told him about WEC's financial struggles and how terrible he felt in those months when no funds came in to send to their missionaries. He knew how much they needed the money.

Next, Norman told Rees about the executive committee and how they were relentless in trying to get C.T. Studd to come home and take up a different leadership role in the mission. Norman hated to think of the direction in which the committee members would take the mission after C.T. died. After Norman poured out his heart, Rees chuckled and told Norman, "Watch out for God. No matter what men try to do, God will never let His servant down. C.T. Studd has been a faithful servant. Expect to step in and carry the mission along the same principles when the time comes."

During Norman's stay in Wales, Rees encouraged him, and they spent much time together in prayer, praying about things other people might misunderstand. By the time he returned to London, Norman knew he'd made a new friend. Whenever he could, he would take the train back to Wales to visit Rees. He deeply valued the man's prayers and advice. And he needed them both in January 1929 when his mother-in-law, Priscilla, died after only one day of illness. Everyone was stunned. The work of carrying on where she had left off fell to Gilbert and Dorothy Barclay and to Norman and Pauline.

It didn't take Norman long to see that the executive committee had been holding back on what they really wanted to say about C.T. Studd out of respect for his wife. Now that she was dead, they felt free to be blunter than ever. They wrote letters telling C.T. that other missionaries reported he was too much of a zealot. Couldn't he go a little easier on the Congolese Christians and not insist on so much holiness?

Norman was appalled. He knew that C.T. would never compromise his standards, and he longed to go to Africa to see if he could help sort things out before a permanent break took place between the London office and the Belgian Congo team. The only reason the executive committee was urging rather than demanding that C.T. come home was that, as founder of the mission, C.T. had the right to veto any of their decisions. According to WEC's bylaws, his vote overrode all others. Norman knew that that situation wouldn't last, that the executive committee would take WEC in a different direction as soon as his father-in-law died, and that they were free to do so.

Around this time, Pauline's widowed sister, Grace, and her second husband, Lieutenant Colonel David Munro, along with their only child, eleven-year-old Ian, came to live in the Studd family home. David was a hero of the Great War. Following the war, he and Grace had emigrated to Rhodesia, where they became farmers. Recently they had sold their farm and returned to England to live and find a good school for Ian. Having them live in the family home, which was also the mission headquarters, was a challenge, especially since David was adamant about having no time for Christianity. He was raised in a Christian home but had drifted away from his childhood faith during the war and declared that he was never going back to it. Norman and the others living at the house prayed regularly for his conversion.

By now, Norman had finished translating the New Testament into the Bangala language and arranged for twenty-thousand copies to be printed by the British and Foreign Bible Society and sent to the Congo.

In late November 1929, Norman set out on a tour to visit the twenty WEC missionaries serving in Amazonia. As he made his way up the Amazon River toward its headwaters and into the Amazon rain forest, Norman was amazed by what he encountered. Even though he had experienced difficult living conditions in the tropical forests of the northeastern Belgian Congo, in a letter to the C.U.M.B. members, Norman noted, "I feel that I have never known what it means to be a pioneer missionary until I went there, and to work in Africa is like being in a comfortable armchair compared to Amazonia."

Norman was transported far upriver in a native canoe to visit the missionaries. Dense jungle grew to the edge of the river on either side, and the five native Christian paddlers would tell Norman when the jungle was uninhabited and when it was the territory of fierce tribes. At night they pulled the canoe to the side of the river, cleared some space for an overnight camp, and cooked their dinner, which consisted mostly of roast monkey.

One particularly moving moment on the trip upriver occurred when they stopped where Fenton Hall's body was buried. Norman thought of Fenton's journal that he had edited and published five years before. Missionaries were now serving in Amazonia and other places around the world because of the journal. And Fenton's death had opened the way for many Amazonian Indians to become Christians.

In May 1930, after five months of traveling throughout the Amazon Basin meeting with and encouraging the WEC missionaries, including his younger brother, Kenneth, Norman returned to Great Britain, deeply impressed by the mission's work in Amazonia.

Back in England, Norman and Pauline felt a great need to see C.T. one last time and assess the current situation in the Belgian Congo. However, the executive committee refused to allow them to go unless they had a direct request from C.T. Pauline and Norman prayed about what to do, and within days a letter arrived from C.T. saying how much he wished he could see them both one more time. That was all Norman and Pauline needed. The money to cover the cost of the trip flowed in, and they set out for Africa in early August 1930.

Once more Norman wrote to the C.U.M.B. members about the experience:

The greatest inspiration of our visit has been to be with Mr. Studd again: he is exceedingly weak, but absolutely refuses to spare himself in spite of all doctors say: he gets up and gives himself right out in the native meeting (which is three hours long at its shortest when he takes it). Has to be helped to his bed, then as soon as well enough he carries on necessary business, then up again for a couple of hours or so over the Bible and in prayer with the missionaries: then out for a week-end in the forest and the same thing: he has such a hold on the natives that [where] six or seven hundred come normally, two thousand come when they hear "The great Bwana" is coming, and they bring food and a bed-mat so as to stay over Sunday night and get an extra dose in the morning!

While in Ibambi, it was obvious to Norman and Pauline and the other WEC missionaries serving in the Congo that C.T. did not have much longer to live. C.T. also seemed to know this and had thought about the future of the mission. He explained to Norman that Jack Harrison, a missionary from Liverpool, was both his and the other missionaries' choice to take over as leader of WEC's work in the Belgian Congo upon his death. And C.T. wanted Norman and Pauline back in London to take over the leadership of WEC and move forward the mission's call to open new mission fields around the world.

In February 1931, before setting out on the long journey home to England, Norman and Pauline said what they were sure was their final goodbye to C.T. Norman carried with him a letter from C.T. stating that he had appointed Norman and Pauline to be his representatives and to take over running of the home office. But even as he traveled home, Norman had doubts about whether the executive committee would accept C.T.'s explicit wishes. He tried not to think about what would happen if they didn't.

Chapter 10

Mission in the Balance

By the time Norman and Pauline got back to 17 Highland Road, Upper Norwood, everyone, from the newest missionary recruit to the old man who cleaned the office, had an opinion as to what should happen with WEC. Norman listened to them all and realized they wanted the same thing—a thriving mission that continued to branch out into new countries with the gospel. Where they disagreed was on how this should happen. Members of the executive committee pointed to the turnover in staff as a major reason why the mission needed to take better care of its missionaries by offering them more support in the field. Norman agreed. He knew that a number of WEC missionaries had become discouraged and joined other missionary organizations, while some

111

had left the mission field altogether. He knew this had to change, but how? The executive committee wanted more rules and regulations put in place along with more meetings, more reports, and more paperwork. But Norman wanted to follow the path C.T. Studd had laid out: trusting God to guide each individual missionary and provide for him or her.

As he pondered the situation, Norman knew there was one man whose advice he trusted more than any other—Rees Howells. As soon as he was able, he took the train from London to Swansea, Wales, to visit Rees and see if he could find a way forward through the mess the mission found itself in. On the night Norman arrived, Rees listened sympathetically as Norman unburdened his heart.

"Do you have the written bylaws of the mission with you?" Rees asked. "I'd like to study them."

Norman nodded and went upstairs to retrieve a copy of the mission's Principles and Practices from his bag. "I'm not sure anything like this will help," he said, handing the copy to Rees. "The executive committee has sidelined Pauline and me and the rest of the Studd children. They say they are taking over now, for the good of the mission."

The following morning, the two men went for a walk in the Welsh countryside. "The Principles and Practices document is pretty clear on what happens if the founder and the executive committee get into a major disagreement," Rees said.

"I know," Norman replied. "The founder has veto power. What he says goes. But C.T. is not here, and the committee insist they have the right to rearrange everything."

"According to the Principles and Practices, they don't. C.T. has the right to say what happens, and since he invested you with his authority in England, you are acting on his behalf as his agent. Am I right?"

Norman nodded wearily. The last thing he wanted was open conflict with the executive committee. At heart he was a man of peace who wanted everyone to get along.

"You're going to have to go back to headquarters and take what belongs to C.T. Studd and his mission—the records, the correspondence, the bankbooks, everything," Rees declared.

Norman took a deep breath. He wasn't pleased with the idea of confronting people, some of whom had been his friends for many years.

"Remember what I told you when you first came to visit me? You must expect when the time comes to step in and carry the mission along the same principles as C.T. Studd. That's the mark of a strong leader."

While he felt far from being a strong leader, as Norman prayed about the situation, he realized the mission was at a crucial point. He, as C.T.'s agent and spokesman in Great Britain, was the only one who could do anything legally about it.

WEC's records were housed at 19 Highland Road, Upper Norwood, next door to the headquarters house. It had once been the stable for the Studd home before it was converted to provide space for missionaries coming from and going to the mission field. The executive committee had already claimed the place as its own.

Back in London, Norman talked to his brother-in-law, David Munro, and together they hatched a plan to remove the records early in the morning and return them to the headquarters house. Everything went better than expected. The committee had changed the locks at house number 19, and Norman and David thought they were going to have to break into the place. To their surprise they discovered the executive committee had hired an older man to clean the rooms before work each morning.

When Norman and David went next door carrying large canvas rucksacks, they discovered that the man was inside the building and had left his keys in the door. Quietly they opened it and walked inside. David pulled out a pocketknife and cut the telephone cord. "That way, if the old man finds us, he won't be able to call anyone from the committee to come and challenge us," he whispered. Despite his nervousness, Norman grinned. Since David had been a colonel during the Great War, he was treating the whole experience like a mission behind enemy lines.

Norman and his brother-in-law stealthily made their way to the room where the records were kept and loaded them into the rucksacks. The whole operation took only several minutes. David told Norman he was certain the old man doing the cleaning at number 19 had no idea the two of them had been inside and removed the records. And if he did, he had no way of calling the committee members to let them know.

Later that morning, Norman wrote to each member of the executive committee, dismissing them from their position on behalf of C.T. Studd. It was over. The committee had no legal grounds upon which to challenge the move. C.T. was still alive, and Norman was his representative.

The members of the committee didn't fight back. Instead they regrouped. By June 29, 1931, they had set up a new missionary society called the Unevangelised Fields Mission (UFM). Soon afterward Norman learned that all eighteen WEC missionaries working in Amazonia had defected to UFM, as had two missionaries in Northern India and half of those working in the Belgian Congo. Norman also received a letter from his brother Kenneth informing him he wanted no part in the WEC split and had taken a job with the Survey Application Trust, a different mission group whose goal was to map unreached areas of South America.

The situation was a great financial burden to Norman. While he was sure that God had spoken to him through Rees and that he was doing the right thing, it came at a great cost. The mission had split in half, the executive committee was dissolved, rumors were flying, churches were taking sides, and some well-known Christian leaders had canceled speaking engagements on behalf of WEC. Faced with these consequences, Norman and Pauline did the only thing they knew with certainty to do—pray.

Early on the morning of Friday, July 17, 1931, two and a half weeks after retrieving the WEC records from the number 19 house, Norman and Pauline kneeled beside their bed praying about the lack of funds. They may have held onto the legal identity of the mission, but it was now a shell of what it had once been. Norman knew there was no way forward unless God intervened. As they prayed, Pauline nudged Norman. He opened his eyes and looked into hers. "Father is gone home," she said. "I know it. We are to start anew with God."

In that instant Norman knew without a doubt that his wife was right. C.T. Studd was dead. The mission was now fully in their hands. The two continued to kneel in silence. Norman wondered how they would take over the work of such a great man of faith.

Norman had just sat down to breakfast when he heard a knock at the door. It was a delivery man with a telegram. Norman looked at Pauline as he tore the envelope open and read aloud. They both already knew what it would say. "Bwana (CT Studd) glorified July 16th."

"He died last night," Pauline said. "How good of God to give us warning."

Two weeks later, Norman and Pauline received a letter from Jack Harrison in the Belgian Congo telling them the details of C.T.'s death and funeral. As he read, Norman could imagine the scene in C.T.'s native hut, with Jack leaning over the old man. Jack wrote, "It was amazing to see him passing out like this—quite conscious all through and just 'Hallelujah' coming out with every breath he had. At about 7 p.m. on Thursday he seemed to lapse into unconsciousness and shortly after 10:30 p.m. passed to his reward. It was a fine passing."

Norman continued reading the letter to Pauline. Jack explained how he and others from Ibambi had worked through the night preparing the coffin. He described how he'd imagined a small burial service in the morning but how, as dawn broke, hundreds of natives had poured into the village on foot, bicycle, and sedan chair. By noon over two thousand people were gathered at C.T.'s graveside. Jack wrote, "The natives who came in on Friday for the burial would not go away again. We had a splendid meeting on Saturday with them, and oh, the prayers! We had never heard the like from blacks before. All seemed to have the same thought in their minds, that of reconsecrating themselves to God. . . . Today also, (Sunday), we have had larger crowds that ever. It is the Lord's doing and marvelous in our eyes."

When he finished reading, Norman turned to Pauline. Tears flowed down their cheeks. "It is a new beginning," Pauline said. "We cannot do this, but we must believe God will bring it to pass."

And so, Norman and Pauline Grubb determined to start over again. Four staff stayed on in the Studd house: Daisy Kingdon, who was home on furlough; Elsie Dexter, a young woman missionary in training; and Grace Walder and Miss Muller, who took care of the secretarial work.

The first change Norman made was in the way they conducted prayer meetings. In the past, headquarters staff had committed to a half-hour prayer meeting each morning, followed by eight hours of mission work. Now that the mission had been so dramatically downsized, Norman explained to his little team that *prayer* was now their work. They would pray as long as God inspired them to do so and fit the rest of the administrative work around that.

As a statement of their faith in God, Norman and Pauline agreed that they would no longer take any of the mission's funds for themselves or their children. Until now, money the mission received supported home missionaries as well as those on the mission field. From now on they would use money sent to them only for the support of foreign missionaries. The staff at home would trust God to provide their food, clothing, and transport.

It took every ounce of Norman's faith to believe that WEC could once more be a vibrant mission organization. C.T. Studd had been known around the world, but now, following the public cleaving of WEC factions, the mission had a poor reputation. In the month since the split, only fifty pounds had been given to support the remaining thirty-five missionaries in the field. This was also due in part to the fact that Great Britain, along with the rest of the Western world, was in the midst of a deep financial depression. Income taxes in England had risen to 25 percent, and almost three million people were out of work. How could the mission build more support for its missionaries when facing such dire circumstances?

In his gloomy moments, Norman wondered if the mission was doomed to fail. Yet letters from missionaries in the Belgian Congo kept the mission moving forward. The letters contained stories of open doors to the gospel such as they had never seen before. Chiefs and headmen throughout the area were opening their lands to the missionaries, and new tribes were being reached. In the Congo the mission was stretched as thin as it could go, and the missionaries begged for more workers to be sent.

Norman realized that WEC needed a representative who could travel throughout Great Britain speaking and stirring up interest in the Belgian Congo. He knew exactly the kind of person they needed—someone who was already familiar with the mission, had served in the Congo with them, and had known C.T. personally. He or she also needed to be a dynamic speaker. The person had to be willing to be on the road for most of the year and willing to do it with no financial support from the mission. Norman knew it was a tall order; he couldn't think of a single person who fit the bill. He didn't want to bring back one of missionaries from the Belgian Congo to take over the responsibility, as their work was too important to interrupt. But who else was there? Norman pondered the question a thousand times.

One evening, not too long after C.T.'s death, Norman was preparing to preach at a meeting in Liverpool. Over a thousand people were seated in the audience waiting to hear him, but when Norman noticed one man in particular in the front row, his heart sank. It was Alfred Ruscoe. Alfred Ruscoe! *Why is he here*? Norman asked himself. He'd hoped never to meet the man again. Alfred had joined C.T. in the heart of Africa in 1920. He was an effective missionary. He gave all he had to the mission and became like a son to C.T. All had gone well until Alfred contracted blackwater fever and returned to England to recuperate. While home recuperating he came under the influence of some of the executive committee members who convinced him that C.T. asked too much of him and that he should not go back to the Congo.

Norman remembered the shock and revulsion he felt when he learned that Alfred had betrayed C.T. and spoken out against WEC in public. Alfred had then joined a more structured mission and returned to Africa to serve with them. And now here he was, sitting ten feet away. Norman was convinced that Alfred was there to undermine the evening's presentation. Nonetheless, he preached with great conviction about the vision God had given C.T. and finished his sermon by reading the last lines of a poem C.T. had written:

> Only one life, 'twill soon be past,
> Only what's done for Christ will last.
> And when I am dying, how happy I'll be,
> If the lamp of my life has been burned out for
>   Thee.

At the end of the meeting Norman expected Alfred Ruscoe to quickly leave the auditorium. Instead Alfred made his way directly to the stage. He was one of the first people in line to shake Norman's hand. To overcome the awkwardness of the moment, Norman asked him, "So what are you doing now?"

"Not much," Alfred replied.

With a nod, Norman quickly said to him, "Then you'd better come and help me."

The two men stared at each other. Norman wasn't sure who was more shocked by the words that had just come out of his mouth. He didn't trust Alfred Ruscoe, and he certainly didn't want him back in the mission at such a fragile time. Yet the words were out.

"I suppose we should talk about it," Alfred said cautiously.

"Yes, yes," Norman agreed, wishing he hadn't said such a stupid thing. "Are you back living near Derby?"

Alfred nodded and then said, "Aren't you going to be preaching there later in the month?"

"I am. We should get together then and talk some more," Norman added.

With that Alfred shook Norman's hand enthusiastically and walked off, leaving Norman to continue greeting the people lined up on the platform to meet him and answer their questions about WEC.

As he left the hall that night, Norman was still wondering what had made him ask Alfred to join them. In human terms it seemed like a potential disaster, yet somewhere deep inside, he wondered if God might be trying to get his attention.

A week and a half later Norman arrived in Derby to speak. The meeting was smaller than the one in Liverpool, and once more he spoke about C.T.'s vision to reach lost souls and challenged those in attendance to follow in his footsteps. After the meeting Alfred approached Norman and said he was interested in rejoining WEC. Norman tried to dissuade him. As they walked to the railway station together to catch their respective trains, the two men agreed to talk more about the matter in the future. But when they reached the station, they discovered that both their trains had already departed.

"There's a café over yonder with a cheap room for rent upstairs, if you two gentlemen want to spend the night and come back in the morning for the next train," the stationmaster suggested.

Norman shrugged his shoulders. He didn't seem to have much choice. He and Alfred carried their bags over to the café and paid for a room. As they climbed the narrow staircase to the room, Norman wondered how he was going to make small talk with this man who'd been so antagonistic to WEC for so long.

Once in the room Norman discovered he didn't need to worry. Alfred was eager to fill Norman in on how he had returned home to England from Africa for good following his third bout of blackwater fever. "About eighteen months ago, God told me He had a special plan for me," Alfred confided to Norman. "I have been doing all I can to find out what it is. I visited Rees Howells in hopes that he could help me."

Norman's ears pricked up at his friend's name. "How was that?" he asked.

"I had a wonderful time of blessing with him," Alfred said. "But I still lacked the direction I thought

I needed, so I decided to become an ordained minister in the Church of England. But now I'm wondering if I am being called to join you at WEC's home office."

Norman didn't reply, and the two men sat in silence a few minutes. They hadn't discussed the new policy wherein all money given to the mission went to support missionaries in the field and home workers had to find their own money to live on. Norman knew that one of Alfred's main complaints had been that C.T. demanded too much self-sacrifice.

Alfred resumed the conversation. "If I were to join you, there's one thing I would have to insist upon. I've been working with the Friend's Evangelistic Band and have had such a blessing living by faith instead of relying on wages that I could not go back to working for an allowance. I could not allow the mission to pay me."

Norman could barely believe what he was hearing. He went over in his mind the things he and Pauline had been praying for in a mission representative—someone who knew the mission and had known C.T., could not return to the Belgian Congo, was a good public speaker, and was called to work for a mission that would not pay him. Alfred fit all the criteria. Norman was utterly surprised. Who would have thought God could change a man's heart so much as He had changed Alfred Ruscoe's?

The two men talked and prayed long into the night, and by morning, when they boarded their trains, Norman was certain that Alfred was God's choice for the job opening at WEC. They agreed that he would join them in Upper Norwood in two weeks. Now Norman and the team in London faced the challenge of what to do with those who were called to join WEC in Africa. The mission currently did not have the money necessary to send them to the mission field or keep them once they got there.

Chapter 11

"What Are You Aiming For?"

In November 1931, Harold Coleman and Frank Cripps departed England to work with WEC in the Belgian Congo. The mission managed to eke out enough money to cover the cost of their passage, but since none was left to purchase the standard equipment new missionaries would take with them, the two men left without it. Norman hoped that sometime in the future the home team in London would be able to ship the equipment to them.

Sending the two men placed a tremendous strain on Norman and Pauline because it paled in comparison to the need for many more missionaries in the Congo. Norman wondered if the mission could even financially sustain sending two missionaries every six months.

The entire home office team, including Norman's brother-in-law, David Munro, who'd just officially joined WEC as its business director, decided to pray until they got some clear direction on how to move forward. Norman was delighted that David was now part of WEC. Despite David's having declared that he would never go back to the Christian faith he had been raised in, when David arrived at the Studd home in Upper Norwood, Norman and others prayed regularly for his conversion. Now David not only was a committed Christian and part of the mission but also had an unswerving commitment to prayer.

One morning in late November 1931, the WEC headquarters team gathered as usual for prayer after breakfast. As they prayed, Norman felt God asking him, "What are you aiming for?" It was an interesting question, one Norman had to admit he didn't have the answer to. And then another question popped into his mind. "What commission did your founder have, which has been passed on to you?" Norman knew the answer to that. Everyone in the room did—to evangelize the world. "Well, are you going to do it or not?" he heard the voice in his mind ask. Norman was instantly flooded with reasons why it was impossible to do. "How did the men of the Bible do the impossible?" came the voice. "By faith," Norman replied.

Norman then asked those present to open their Bibles and read to themselves the story of Joshua following the death of Moses. God had spoken to Joshua and told him to go forward, and to be strong and courageous. Joshua then called together his officers and told them to prepare food because they would cross the Jordan River in three days.

As each member of the home staff silently read the story and contemplated its meaning, a moment of insight flashed through Norman's mind: *If I have the faith and declare a timeline for growth in the mission, God will do the rest. He wants me to believe He can do it. It's not up to me at all. It's up to God!"*

Norman repeated the insight aloud. "The question is, Are we willing to trust God to turn our mission around and support more missionaries?"

Several people nodded in agreement. "Then let's ask God what timeline we should set and how many more missionaries we should believe Him to raise up." With that, the group began to pray some more.

"I believe God wants us to claim ten missionaries to be recruited and trained by July, the first anniversary of C.T. Studd's death," someone finally spoke up.

Yesterday Norman would have dismissed the idea as impossible. Today he had faith to believe it would happen. Not counting Harold and Frank, the mission had seven months for God to send eight more missionaries to the Belgian Congo, whom they needed to train, cover travel costs for, and provide with basic equipment. Norman calculated it would cost the mission at least two thousand pounds to do this. He almost laughed aloud at the audacity of the amount. The previous month, after paying their bills and buying food, the mission had less than one pound left. And now here they were, believing God to send them two thousand pounds in addition to what they needed to keep the office in London afloat. Yet when he got up from his knees, Norman felt invigorated. He had a new sense of direction. He was sure everyone else in the room did too. It was time to rebuild the mission and forge ahead with God's promises rather than keep their eyes on the economic depression happening around them.

The next day, instead of praying for help, the staff at WEC's home office thanked God for the ten missionaries He was raising up. Norman realized he should write straightaway to Jack Harrison to let him know to expect eight more missionary recruits besides Harold and Frank. The missionaries already serving in the Congo would need to build huts to house them and gather various supplies. Then doubt crept in. *Wouldn't it be better to wait until some of the new recruits have applied or some of the money has come in? Won't I look foolish if this doesn't happen?* Norman recognized this immediately as a test of his faith and quickly wrote the letter to Jack, placed it in an envelope, and put it in the mailbox at the end of the street before he could talk himself out of it.

As he walked back to the house, Norman thought of a proverb he had heard in Africa: "If a man plants a garden and dies, his children eat of the fruit." *Yes,* he thought. *C.T. Studd, Bwana, planted for God. We shall enter in and reap the harvest.*

Christmas 1931 came and went. All of Pauline's sisters came to the family home in Upper Norwood to celebrate. Altogether they had nine children between the ages of three and twelve, and the house was filled with the pitter-patter of little feet running up and down the stairs. In the back garden the adults and children played cricket and other games. Each of the Studd women remarked on how much their mother would have loved to have been there with them all. That Christmas Norman keenly felt the absence of both Priscilla and C.T.

Early in 1932, three young women—Elsie Brown, Lily Peckett, and Annie Rose—applied to go to the Congo with WEC. They all seemed strong candidates, and Norman invited them to stay in the mission house next door at 19 Highland Road for training and so people could get to know them. By Easter, everyone living in the Studd house and the next-door mission house agreed that the three women were strong in their faith and ready to go to the Belgian Congo as soon as possible. There was just that one nagging, recurring problem—a lack of money.

Before the women set off to attend an Easter convention, those at WEC headquarters prayed that the money would come in during the convention. Norman expected that some Christians at the convention would give toward meeting the need, but that was not how things worked out.

Two older women came to stay in the mission house for Easter weekend, and Norman and Pauline were glad to have them. The two women understood the challenges of living by faith, because they too lived the same way. At a prayer meeting over the weekend, one of the WEC staff members mentioned that 450 pounds was needed to send the three missionary recruits to the Congo. The next morning the two guests arrived at breakfast very excited. "God spoke to us in the night, each of us separately!" one of the women said. "Yes," the other woman said, "and He told us both the same thing."

Norman waited to hear what it was.

"We've had some money in a bank account for several years. There are many good causes we wanted to spend it on, but every time we went to withdraw it, God told us, no. He had a special purpose for it," the first woman said.

"And last night He told us both to give it to you to send the three new missionaries to the Belgian Congo," the second woman added.

It was enough to cover equipment and the cost of travel to the Congo for two of the recruits. By the end of day, the rest of the money had arrived in the form of a donation from a Christian women's group in London. Now all three young women could set out together.

Two months later, on May 26, the three missionary recruits boarded a train at London's Victoria Station to begin their long journey to the Congo. Fifty WEC staff and supporters were there to see them off.

Soon afterward, Norman received some sad news. His younger brother, Kenneth, had been visiting Spain and Portugal doing research on Central America when his wife, Eileen, joined him in Seville, Spain. Soon after her arrival, she became ill and died, leaving Kenneth a widower with their two young sons, a four-year-old and an eleven-month-old, to care for. Kenneth took time off to grieve the loss of his wife before returning to his work in South America, leaving his two sons in the care of their maternal grandparents in the west of England.

As Norman and his family grieved their loss, more prospective missionaries applied to work with WEC. Two Englishmen, Vernon Willson and Stephen Cottam, and a Canadian woman, Irene James, came to spend time at WEC headquarters in London. Once again the workers at the home office set to praying for God to release the money needed to equip and send the new missionaries. They experienced some moments when they all had to dig deep into their faith that God would provide, but the three new missionaries set out for the Belgian Congo on June 16, 1932. Norman was humbled. Great Britain was still in the grip of a financial crisis, yet the mission had been able to equip and send eight missionaries in the past seven months. They needed only two more to fulfill the vision of sending ten missionaries to the Belgian Congo by July 16, 1932, the first anniversary of C.T.'s death.

The last two new missionary recruits were Rose Sore, a trained nurse, and Ivor Davies, a graduate of Rees Howells's Bible college in Wales. They had applied before the anniversary of C.T.'s death but did not set out for the Congo until August 10. With their departure, everyone in WEC was elated. Norman wrote the following to the C.U.M.B. members:

> We felt led to ask God to start us off by sending us ten fully-trained new workers for Africa

and the full funds for sending them out by the anniversary of Mr. Studd's death. They came, the exact number and the full sum completed five days before the date. Ten seems a small number, considering the difficulties with which we were faced a year ago, we knew we were asking the impossible when we began to pray, and the coming of the Ten to us is as wonderful a miracle as a much larger number to a bigger mission. . . . The translation work into Bangala has been carried on between whiles, and Psalms are now in print, and the Old Testament extracts go to press [God willing] at the end of this month.

In March 1933, Norman reported to C.U.M.B. members that his translation work, which had taken up most of his spare time, was now complete. He had already moved on to a new task. In this letter Norman wrote, "I have begun collecting and sorting the letters and papers concerning C.T. Studd's life, with a view to writing about it. He and his mother were devoted to each other beyond the average and as a result she has stored up a large and useful correspondence. As I can only do this in my spare time, it will be Christmas before I can put it out, but I believe the book will be a call to many to uttermost abandonment to Christ."

As Norman pointed out, C.T.'s mother had saved all of her son's letters since his days as a cricketer, and his wife, Priscilla, had done the same thing. But as he pored over the letters, Norman realized they didn't contain much information about C.T.'s childhood or teenage years. This was a problem, since he wanted to write about his father-in-law's entire life. He prayed about how best to resolve the situation, but nothing seemed to come to mind or was revealed to him. Norman was just about to give up on the project when Pauline remembered that there was a cupboard in the basement where she'd once seen some old papers.

Norman ran downstairs hoping this was his answer. He found the cupboard after pushing aside an old cabinet. The cupboard hinges were rusty, and he had to pry the door open. Inside was a hodge-podge of books, boxes, and parcels wrapped in brown paper and tied with string. Norman's heart raced as he pulled out the first box, labeled "C.T. School Report Cards." Underneath the box was an envelope marked, "Charlie aged 1." Norman opened the envelope and inside was a lock of golden hair. He felt like dancing! Here it was, a treasure trove of information and mementos he needed to complete the biography. They had been in the basement all along.

The cupboard was crammed from floor to ceiling, and it took Norman six weeks to go through it all. He found a cache of historic letters from General William Booth, D. L. Moody, Hudson Taylor and George Müller. Each letter offered a fascinating glimpse into the work of these great men and their relationship with C.T. Studd.

One thing was not progressing, however. The mission had committed to praying for fifteen new missionary recruits to go to the Belgian Congo by the second anniversary of C.T.'s death in July 1931. By now it was March 1933, and in the eight months since the announcement had been made, three young men had been sent, but there were no other applicants. Norman began to doubt. They needed to send twelve more missionaries in just four months. Was that possible? Had they heard God's voice wrong?

The question haunted Norman, until one day he sat talking with a visitor at the mission house. "What makes you think all of the missionaries have to be sent to the Belgian Congo? Didn't I read somewhere that C.T. Studd had a vision of his mission reaching the whole world?" the man asked.

Norman was stunned. Why hadn't he thought of that? At the time of the mission split two years before, those missionaries serving with WEC in other parts of the world had left to serve with other missions. Given this, and the fact the Belgian Congo was WEC's founding mission field, had caused Norman to put the focus of the mission back on the Congo as they regrouped. In fact, the London office had received letters and inquiries from Christians wanting to serve with WEC in other places in the world, but they had been turned away. Norman suddenly realized it was he, not God, who had put in place the condition that all fifteen new missionary recruits should go to the Belgian Congo. It was true, God had spoken to C.T. Studd to evangelize the world, and it was time for WEC to focus on mission fields beyond the Congo.

Soon after Norman came to this realization, a young Australian man named Pat Symes showed up at WEC headquarters, certain that God was calling him to work in Colombia, the least-evangelized country in South America. Norman was also sure and set about helping Pat prepare to serve with WEC in Colombia. Within weeks a Welsh woman named Nesta Evans also applied to serve in Colombia. Now two WEC missionaries were preparing to head out for that country.

Soon the floodgates opened, and new recruits applied to serve in Arabia, while two more applied to go to Spanish Guinea, on the western equatorial coast of Africa. Then Ivy Roberts applied to go to the Congo, where her brother and sister already served with WEC. Rex and Julia Bavington and Daniel Voumard were next, all three available for missionary service in Baltistan, or Little Tibet, along India's mountainous norther border with China.

Life at WEC headquarters in London soon became quite hectic as these young men and women trained and prepared to work in various countries and cultures. It was difficult to research some of these areas, as they were closed to most Westerners. Staff members at the home office were kept busy praying and asking God to provide the money to get new recruits to the places they were called. At times, as they waited, Norman would feel a little stressed. But the money always arrived just in time, and soon WEC missionaries were traveling to far-flung places around the world.

Six weeks before the second anniversary of C.T.'s death, however, applications for missionary service with WEC stopped abruptly, two missionaries and five hundred pounds short of reaching their goal.

On July 15, 1933, Norman and Pauline went to the Worldwide Evangelization Crusade Conference being hosted by Rees Howells in Wales. When Norman arrived at the train station in Wales, he was informed that two of the Bible college's students, Harold Wood and John Harbison, had received a call from God to go to Colombia and serve with WEC. Norman was delighted. It was the day before the anniversary of C.T.'s death. All that was now needed was five hundred pounds to equip and send the two young men. Norman prayed about the need and claimed the words of the verse John 15:7: "If you abide in me, and my words abide in you, ye shall ask what ye you will, and it shall be done unto you." As far as Norman knew, he was abiding in God and needed five hundred pounds to send the two new recruits to join the other missionaries in the field.

Throughout the rest of the week, Norman prayed and believed that the money would somehow come in, but it did not. Downhearted, Norman and Pauline climbed into a taxi with several others to ride back to the train station. About halfway to their destination they heard a loud bang. The left rear tire of the taxi had burst. Everyone got out of the vehicle and walked to the nearest tram station to catch a tram, which took them the remaining mile and a half to the train station. But they arrived too late. Their train had already departed. Norman and Pauline and the others bought tickets for the next train to London. As they sat and waited, one of the men who'd been riding in the taxi motioned Norman aside.

The man led Norman outside, and the two of them began walking along the street together. "You know," the man said as they walked, "it's remarkable we both missed the train and are stuck here together. Yesterday the Lord told me that if you still needed money for the last two missionaries, I was to write you a check for four hundred pounds. I tried to ignore the whole idea and leave the conference without seeing you, but here we are. I feel I must speak up and give you the money."

Norman couldn't stop the grin that was spreading across his face. Receiving the money was great, but even greater was the thought that God had answered his prayer—or most of it—in the nick of time.

As they walked the two men found themselves outside a grocery store that a friend of Norman's managed. "Let's go in and tell our brother how God answers prayer!" Norman said, opening the shop door and leading the way in.

At the back of the store, Norman found his friend and related how he'd just received four hundred pounds to send two men as missionaries to Colombia. When he had finished, the manager said, "As you were speaking, God told me I'm to add one hundred pounds to that amount."

The five hundred pounds was all there and had been given between the time the taxi's tire had burst and the tram had arrived at the station to take them to London.

Chapter 12

Bursting at the Seams

C.T. Studd, Cricketer and Pioneer, Norman's biography of his father-in-law, was published in time for Christmas 1933. The publisher told Norman he had high hopes that the book would sell as many as ten thousand copies in ten years. Five months later it had already sold ten thousand copies and was in the process of being reprinted. Norman was delighted, especially when he began to receive letters from all over the world from people inspired by the book. As a result, a new influx of missionary candidates applied to serve with WEC in both new and established mission fields.

WEC was growing fast, and Norman felt it was time to start over in Canada and the United States, establishing a base where missionary candidates could be trained. But who should be the person to lead the new work? It was a difficult assignment, given that WEC had already made one false start in the United States in 1925 when it trained and sent out seven missionaries to serve alongside C.T. in the Belgian Congo. Conflict resulted in the seven missionaries leaving WEC and joining other missions.

As Norman prayed about who should lead this North American expansion, he became convinced that Alfred Ruscoe was the man for the job. Since rejoining WEC, Alfred had done an outstanding job traveling and speaking around the United Kingdom, raising funds and recruiting missionary candidates. When Norman talked to Alfred about reestablishing WEC in Canada and the United States, Alfred wasn't sure he was up to the task. Norman asked him to pray and consider the position. It was four months before Alfred became convinced that God was calling him to go to North America.

In the meantime, a new group of WEC missionaries traveled to Nepal to open a missionary work there. In 1935, twenty-five new missionaries began serving with WEC, and the following year the number of new recruits doubled. Money poured into WEC's home office to support the missionaries in the field. One donor sent a check for five thousand pounds.

Reports from Alfred were encouraging. He was focusing first on Canada, where he'd established a WEC base in Toronto. He intended to move on to the United States once the Toronto base was well established.

In Great Britain, the home office in London was beginning to burst at the seams. Norman realized the mission needed more housing for missionaries-in-training and for those coming and going on furlough. By now WEC occupied three houses in London: 17 Highland Road, C.T. and Priscilla Studd's old home; the stables next door at 19 Highland Road, which over the years had been transformed into office space along with a dormitory loft for eight men; and an equipment storage area. In addition, a friend of WEC had purchased 34 Highland Road across the street and donated it to the mission for use as a guesthouse. In the previous five years, WEC headquarters had gone from housing five people to forty-five. Twelve were permanent staff living and working at the headquarters without salary. The rest were mostly new missionary recruits who, after attending various Bible schools, had come to stay at headquarters long enough to understand their missionary role and for WEC staff to make sure they were up to the task ahead of them.

While overcrowding at the home office was evident to Norman and the other staff, it wasn't until one morning in April 1935 that they began praying for guidance on how to deal with the situation.

Three weeks later, a neighbor visited Norman to discuss the exact boundary line between his property and the stable. Since neither man was certain of the answer, the neighbor offered to do some research at the county council office. He called Norman a week later with new information. "I thought you might like to know that while I was going through the property records, I learned that the stable is located on one of only two lots on which the London county council will allow a new building to be erected."

"How so?" Norman asked.

"I was told that because the only building currently listed as occupying the lot is a stable, it can be demolished and a house built in its place," the neighbor answered.

Norman hung up the phone and sat thinking for a long time. Was it a coincidence that after more than twenty years the mission had just learned this information about the stable property, or was God at work? He kept his eyes and ears open to see what might happen next.

Within a month, an elderly Christian man, who, for many years had supported C.T. Studd and the mission, died. He left WEC a modest house north of London, along with twelve hundred pounds in cash to maintain it. When Norman read the details of the man's will, he learned it allowed for the house to be sold, so long as the proceeds from the sale were used to buy another building for WEC.

Amazingly, within two months of starting to pray about the housing crisis at mission headquarters in London, Norman knew they could demolish the stable and erect a larger structure, and they now had the means to begin the work. There was great excitement in Upper Norwood as members of the mission staff exchanged ideas for the new building. They settled upon a three-story house that would sleep thirty people, have kitchen and dining facilities for sixty, and provide a meeting room that could hold one hundred.

The house bequeathed to WEC in North London sold for two thousand pounds, enough to pay for about half the amount that Leslie Sutton, his old friend from Cambridge and now WEC's building overseer, thought it would cost to build the new structure. As Norman delved into the numbers, he realized Leslie had estimated that half of the four thousand pounds needed for the new building would be spent on labor. *What if*, he began to think, *they could find skilled bricklayers and carpenters, plumbers and electricians willing to donate their time to build the new structure?*

In some ways that felt like an even bigger leap of faith than believing God to provide the full amount of cash needed, but Norman was sure it was the right thing to do. At each morning prayer meeting, the home team began thanking God for the men He would send to help with the construction. One of the men living at mission headquarters was John Byer, an experienced bricklayer. He pointed out that the mission might have difficulty getting the scaffolding necessary to build a three-story structure. Most builders owned their own scaffolding and other construction equipment and were probably unwilling to lend or rent it for use on a project they weren't being paid to build. John knew a Christian contractor at Gravesend named Will Hopkins and offered to write to him to see if he had any ideas as to how they might get some scaffolding and other construction equipment.

Several days later Will showed up at WEC head-quarters. Norman spoke with him and showed him the stable and explained what they wanted to do on the site. Will asked a number of questions regarding the new structure, but as far as Norman was concerned, he seemed far more interested in hearing stories about C.T. Studd and the founding of the mission. While the conversation was lively and interesting, Norman didn't expect to hear from Will again. It was obvious he was a busy man with many building contracts to manage.

To his surprise, a week later Norman received a phone call from Will, who explained to Norman that when he returned home to Gravesend after visiting WEC headquarters he became ill and had spent almost a week in bed. As he lay in bed, he recounted how God had spoken to him about a new building he was about to take on. In his mind he clearly heard God ask him, "The hostel or the contract?" For the rest of the week, Will had wrestled with the question until, as he told Norman, he felt obliged to help with the building. This didn't just mean that he was going to loan the mission his scaffolding, concrete mixer, and other equipment, but that he would personally undertake the oversight of the building project. He would have his architect draw up plans for the structure, and he would obtain the building materials necessary at cost price for the mission without adding a profit margin for himself. Norman gladly accepted Will's offer. At the end of the phone call, Norman rushed to tell the staff what had happened. They all knelt together to thank God for sending Will Hopkins to them.

The building project got off to a slow start. Two years passed before the London county council approved plans for the new house. By the time they did, in January 1937, six skilled men, three carpenters, and three bricklayers had joined the staff at WEC and were ready and waiting to put their skills to work. The men were joined by six others who had no building experience but felt called to undertake labor jobs around the site.

Once the old stable had been demolished, the next task was to dig a hole for the basement and deep foundations for the walls. Using picks and shovels the men set to work. The work was backbreaking, and Norman was surprised by how joyfully the men went about it. Even when their hands blistered, they sang and joked among themselves. And when trucks loaded with bricks arrived, the men formed a chain, passing the bricks from one to the other until they had been removed from the truck and stacked on the building site.

By the end of the month, the enormity of what they were attempting was driven home to Norman when two hundred steel girders arrived at the construction site. The men unloaded and positioned them beside the seventy thousand bricks they'd previously unloaded. Because Will thought that the structure would be much stronger with steel girders, deep concrete supports were erected to bear the weight.

Once the supports were ready, Norman wondered how the girders were going to be lifted into place and who was going to do it, since none of the men on the construction site had experience with them. That is, until Kenneth Cairns arrived at WEC headquarters. Kenneth was from Canada and a new missionary recruit. He was visiting headquarters in Upper Norwood on his way to attend Bible school in preparation for becoming a missionary. Soon after his arrival, Norman sat down with Kenneth to chat and get to know him. He was taken by surprise when he learned that among other things, Kenneth had experience erecting steel girders on construction sites. When he heard of the need, Kenneth agreed to delay the start of his Bible school studies by several weeks so that he could oversee the installation.

Under Kenneth's guidance, the men erected a thirty-three-foot-tall pole to serve as a crane for lifting and maneuvering the girders. Within a month they were set in place. It was time to move on to the next step, the brickwork. At the same time as the bricklayers laid the seventy thousand bricks, the girders were encased in cement to comply with London county council fire regulations. Fireproof floors were then laid on top of them.

Throughout summer 1937 the construction team worked on the project from eight in the morning until eight-thirty at night, far longer hours than bricklayers, laborers, and other skilled construction workers normally worked. Since it was such a dry summer, they wanted to get as much done as possible before winter arrived.

As the job progressed, the building inspector from the London county council made weekly inspection visits. Norman was aware that this man had the power to order any alteration he liked if he did not approve of the quality of work being done. Since alterations were costly, Norman prayed that God would show them favor in the eyes of the building inspector. As he prayed, he watched the inspector, who was gruff and suspicious, begin to soften. As time went on, he became more of a friendly adviser to the men instead of a critic of their work. In fact, he told Norman he was impressed by the quality of work the ragtag group of men on the construction site were producing. Their work was of higher quality than a number of building projects he was inspecting. Norman thanked God for this. From the start of the project, one of the objectives had been to produce first-class work that could withstand the close examination of a picky building inspector.

Once the shell of the building had been erected, the electrical system needed to be designed and installed. No one on the construction team was an electrician, but just as Kenneth Cairns had shown up when someone with girder experience was needed, Michael Lishmund and Leslie Seaman showed up at WEC headquarters. They arrived as new missionary recruits, and both were electrical engineers. Together they designed and installed the electrical system for the new building.

At the end of the summer, Will sent two of his trained workmen to the building site to help with the installation of the roof. Once the roof was finished, forty steel window frames that would hold four hundred panes of glass were fitted to the building. At the same time, work began on the plumbing. Snaking through the walls, water and drain pipes connected the central heating system to radiators in various rooms and hot and cold water to the kitchen, two bathrooms, two shower baths, five toilets, and eight washbasins.

As work continued, Norman oversaw the growth and development of WEC. New missionary recruits continued to apply for service on the many mission fields WEC now facilitated. This kept the home office staff busy getting to know and assessing the suitability of new recruits, training and equipping them for missionary service. And they prayed constantly that God would continue providing the money necessary to carry out their work.

In early spring 1938 work began on painting and decorating the interior of the new building. As had happened throughout the construction process, God continued to send qualified people to Upper Norwood to help. One of these was Australian Trevor White, an interior decorator. He immediately went to work, and after he had finished painting ceilings, walls, and wainscoting from the first floor to the third, linoleum was laid in the rooms and passageways of the upper floors. Oak blocks were used on the floors of the downstairs rooms, and a special cement-like finish was spread on the kitchen floor. After the floor coverings were installed, cabinets were built throughout the place, and large stoves were moved into the kitchen.

By the beginning of June 1938, the new hostel building was finished and ready for residents. Norman was thankful to God for the money and materials that had allowed them to complete the task. He was also humbled by the number of people who had worked on the project for free. And he was indebted to Will Hopkins for his tireless effort in guiding and overseeing the project.

As he walked the hostel one last time before people began moving in, Norman wrote that he felt like he was on holy ground. The faith and love of God and of those who worked on the project was evident on every surface.

A few days later Norman set out on a trip to Canada and the United States, where he visited and traveled with Alfred and spoke in churches and venues. By now Alfred had established a thriving WEC center in Toronto, Canada, that trained missionary recruits, many of whom were now serving with WEC in various parts of the world. Norman was impressed with Alfred's effort and determination.

While in North America, Norman helped establish two WEC centers in the United States, one in Charlotte, North Carolina, and another in Seattle, Washington. After traveling and ministering in Canada and the United States, he moved on to Colombia to inspect WEC's work there. What he saw impressed him. WEC had been working in Colombia for six years, and already thirty-five missionaries were serving with the mission there. They had established a small indigenous church and a Bible school. Norman heard local Christians recount to him amazing stories of how their lives had changed since the missionaries had arrived with the gospel.

Ten months after setting out on his trip, forty-four-year-old Norman arrived back at WEC headquarters in London in March 1939, amazed at how much his children had grown in his absence. Upon his return, Norman began worrying about what was happening in Europe. Once more dark clouds of war seemed to be gathering over the continent. Under the iron-fisted leadership of Adolf Hitler and the Nazis, Germany had militarized and was threatening its neighbors. Norman knew it was a dangerous situation, and it finally exploded on September 1, 1939, when German troops invaded neighboring Poland. In retaliation, two days later, on September 3, British Prime Minister Neville Chamberlain declared war on Germany, as did France.

It was a little more than twenty years since the Great War had ended. That was a war Norman had eagerly fought in. Now, though, he had doubts about whether it was a Christian's duty to fight in such wars. He wrote to the C.U.M.B members about his changing attitude.

Our early members were recruited from the leavings of the last war, and we surely never thought we should see another. . . .

For myself, I fought in the last war; but God has shown me clearly in the past three years the truth of those words "My kingdom is not of this world: if my Kingdom were of this world, then would my servants fight." I see the truth that I now belong to "a holy nation," and spiritual kingdom, already in existence and drawn out of all earthly nations and kingdoms, whose weapons are meekness, love, faith and testimony. So under no circumstances could I take up earthly arms. But I say that humbly knowing that many of God's faithful servants take an opposite view, and I would never wish any view on such a matter to hinder full fellowship in Christ with all my brethren.

The Lord had also made it plain to us as a mission that we were to go right on with our higher warfare for the evangelization of the world. So we have regarded these times of crisis as a special opportunity for proving the promises of God, and launched out in faith for advance and supply of existing needs.

As fighting erupted across Europe and other parts of the world, Norman wondered how WEC could thrive during another war. Would their missionary endeavors be engulfed by the Nazis and their allies? And how many young men now serving in WEC or who wished to join WEC would instead be called up to fight and die for their country?

Chapter 13

Growing Mission in a Turbulent World

The British government again turned to conscription to quickly build up military manpower. Men between the ages of eighteen and forty-one were drafted to fight, though there were some exceptions, such as the sick and disabled and men involved in essential work, including doctors and men whose expertise was needed to keep the country running and producing clothing, food, weapons, and ammunition.

Another category exempted from the draft included monks, priests, or anyone in Holy Orders. Much to Norman's surprise and delight, in this category the British government included men in missionary training at WEC, along with those already serving with the mission in foreign lands. This meant that WEC's overseas workers could carry on with their missionary work instead of going to war. However, Norman knew many promising young men who either volunteered or were drafted to fight. Among them were four of his nephews, George, Richard, and Charles Barclay and Lionel Buxton. Norman's own sons, fifteen-year-old Paul and eleven-year-old Daniel, were both too young to fight.

At first, most of the war action occurred at sea or in Eastern Europe, where the Germans bombed Poland mercilessly, consolidating control over the country. In Great Britain and France, there was little visible military activity on land. In fact, from the declaration of war in September 1939 until May 1940, there was so little action in Western Europe that the newspapers began referring to the war as the "Phoney War." The French and British used this time to train the men they'd drafted, establish defensive positions, and put in place a naval blockade of German ports.

In Great Britain, the government prepared for all-out German air attacks. Civil defense plans were put in place, including blackouts in and around the towns and villages of Great Britain. This would make it more difficult for German pilots to spot bombing targets. Outdoor lights after dusk were banned, and heavy curtains or blankets were draped over windows so that no light from inside houses or buildings could be seen. Cars stopped traveling at night because drivers could no longer use headlights in the dark. At WEC headquarters in Upper Norwood, each night Norman and the other staff members made sure their houses were completely blacked out before they met together to pray about the war in Europe.

Things rapidly changed in spring 1940, when Germany invaded Norway on April 9. Then in May, the German Luftwaffe (air force) began bombing northern France, while German troops captured Luxembourg and then marched into the Netherlands and Belgium. French and British troops rallied to help the Dutch and Belgian armies, but the Germans proved too powerful, overrunning the countries and pushing the French and British Allied forces back into France. The fighting was fierce, and by the end of May, German forces had cut off and surrounded over 300,000 Allied troops near the port of Dunkirk, in northeastern France. The British launched a feverish attempt to evacuate as many as possible of the trapped Allied soldiers.

While Allied troops were being evacuated from Dunkirk, the Germans continued their march into France. French troops offered resistance, but the better equipped German military soon overran them. On June 22, 1940, France surrendered to Nazi Germany.

Following the fall of France, the citizens of Great Britain, including the staff at WEC headquarters, waited anxiously to see what Hitler would do next. They got their answer on September 7, 1940, when wave after wave of German aircraft—over three hundred bombers escorted by six hundred fighter planes—crossed the English Channel. Church bells all over London rang out in warning, and a huge dogfight between the German Luftwaffe and the British Royal Air Force ensued in the skies above London and the Thames Estuary. Many German planes succeeded in dropping their bombs, and on the ground in London, buildings caught fire and smoke filled the streets as the bombs exploded.

When the fight was over and the smoke had cleared, thousands of homes in east and southeast London were reduced to rubble. Four hundred thirty residents of London were dead, and sixteen hundred were seriously injured. The smoldering ruins made it easy for German bombers to target London the next day, and the day after that. This onslaught soon became known as the Blitz, the German word for lightning.

Night after night massive bombs fell on London, reverberating through the city streets, causing building to shake on their foundations. At WEC headquarters on Highland Road the windows were boarded up and the radios tuned to the BBC for the latest news reports.

In the Studd house, Norman and the rest of his family waited anxiously for news of their nephews now swept up in the fighting. It was Norman's brother-in-law, Alfred Buxton, however, who became the first family casualty of the war. On October 14, 1940, Alfred and his brother Murray were attending a committee meeting at Church House Westminster, the London headquarters of the Church of England. They were meeting to discuss publication of a revised translation of the Bible in Amharic, the main language of Ethiopia. During the meeting, Church House was hit by a German bomb. Alfred was killed instantly, as were his brother and four other men.

Norman grieved the death of his forty-eight-year-old brother-in-law. He would never forget how in 1914, at age of twenty-one, Alfred had given up a promising medical career to join C.T. Studd in the Belgian Congo. Despite the fact that many people laughed, saying one of them was too old and one too young for the task they were setting out upon, Alfred and C.T. stuck together for fourteen years building the mission, before C.T. dismissed him. And even then, Alfred had gone on to found another mission in Africa. Soon after hearing of his brother-in-law's death, Norman began writing a biography of Alfred Buxton.

At WEC headquarters Norman encouraged the staff as they redoubled their effort to send out more missionaries and support those already on the mission field. Since no one knew how or when the war would end, it became even more important that they spread the gospel far and wide while they still could.

In late 1940 Norman traveled to Wales to visit Rees. When he arrived, he learned that most of the male students from Rees's Bible college had been conscripted to serve in the military. However, a dedicated group of Christians, mainly women, had stayed on with Rees and his wife, Elizabeth. Together they had turned the Bible college into a house of prayer. Each evening from seven o'clock until midnight, and often later, everyone met to pray, and at least once a week they prayed all day. Rees led the group in what he called "intersession." By this he meant they all sat in silence until someone felt God urging him or her to pray for something specific. Then the group would pray until they believed God had heard and answered their prayers, even if they could not yet see evidence of it.

Rees told Norman how the group had been interceding for the British and French troops stranded at Dunkirk. The group prayed and prayed until they felt God had heard their prayers and was going to make a way to evacuate the men, despite the Germans bearing down on them. On May 28, 1940, the English Channel, across which the men needed to be ferried to safety, was perfectly calm, something locals said they hadn't seen or heard of in a hundred years. At the same time a violent storm arose around the stranded troops, grounding the German fighter planes that had been bombing them from above. Given these conditions, the British began a massive evacuation of troops from Dunkirk, which Norman had read about in the newspapers. The evacuation lasted nine days and involved 860 ships, including around 700 small boats. In all they rescued 338,226 soldiers from France, ferrying them to safety in England. "We continue to intercede for England and her Allies every day," Rees told Norman. "We believe the Holy Spirit is stronger than the devil in the Nazi system. This is the battle of the ages, and victory here means victory for millions of people." Norman later learned that this would not be the only battle during World War II that turned to the advantage of the Allies through the prayers and intercession of Rees Howells and his team of intercessors.

Norman left Wales feeling energized and challenged. At the beginning of the war he'd prayed boldly that God would give WEC a stronger presence at home so that the mission could recruit and send out more missionaries. After visiting Rees, Norman felt now was the time to make that happen. During the annual staff conference at WEC headquarters in January 1941, Norman spread a large map of the United Kingdom on a dining room table in front of the forty-six staff members in attendance. He then told them to pray and ask God where other WEC home bases should be located throughout the country.

By the end of the conference, Norman felt they had a clear path forward. Together they decided to plant eleven regional WEC home bases in the United Kingdom—two in Ireland, two in Scotland, one in Wales, two in Northern England, three in the Midlands, and one in the south—while maintaining the headquarters office in London. Norman and the staff declared in faith that eight of the new centers would be up and running by January of the following year.

The next edition of the WEC newsletter showed a map of the United Kingdom with the proposed centers and asked Christians who felt called to staff them to step forward. Norman made it clear that the WEC centers were not to be in competition with local churches. He wrote, "They are to have no membership, to hold no Sunday services, do nothing which would possibly constitute them as churches; but they are to be humble servants of and co-operators of all Christ's servants and all churches in their towns, they are to help forward or initiate all kinds of co-operative evangelism: help all mission societies."

After the staff conference, Norman and Leslie Sutton embarked upon a speaking tour of England. As they traveled and spoke, they were constantly on the lookout for Christians who felt called to help open the regional centers. Before long the two men found themselves sitting in a Sunday school room at a church in Colchester, northwest of London, with Ken and Bessie Adams.

"Tell me why you wanted to meet with us," Norman asked Ken.

"It's about the map you published in the latest WEC newsletter showing the locations of proposed WEC outreach centers in Great Britain. We saw you want a center in Norwich. Would you consider Colchester instead? You see, we run our own independent Christian bookshop here in Colchester. Bessie and I thought we could offer a WEC worker room and board to help get the center set up, if you would consider locating in our town."

"That's what *we* were thinking before we started to pray," Bessie interjected, a twinkle in her eye.

"Quite right," her husband continued. "As we prayed, the Lord made it plain we were to offer ourselves to be the WEC workers in Colchester. I know we'd need more training. I did missionary training in Scotland in hopes of going to Spain to spread the gospel, but of course the civil war there changed all that. Instead, I went to Cornwall to work in home missions. And then I ended up moving to Colchester and opening the bookstore."

"Ken and I met in Cornwall." Bessie beamed as she spoke. "God had called me to work with the Friends

Evangelistic Band in small English villages. We got married, and Ken joined the band with me. For the next few years we traveled around Britain, taking the gospel to all sorts of villages and towns. Sometimes we took with us whatever Christian literature we could find and set up a table to distribute it."

"Yes, and the more books we carried with us, the more people bought. It didn't take long for us to realize that providing good Christian literature went hand in hand with evangelism," Ken added.

Norman nodded as he recalled that Leslie and WEC's artist, Charlton Smith, had often prayed aloud at meetings about the need for the mission to have a literature arm. Norman looked over at Leslie, who was listening intently to the conversation.

"There is just one problem," Ken continued. "As I told you, we run a Christian bookstore, The Bible Depot. We have prayed and prayed about selling it or finding someone to run it for us, but we can't find any peace about either option. The bookstore has been a great blessing to people in the area. There's nothing else like it. Somehow, we can't imagine that it's God's will to close it down." Then taking a deep breath, Ken looked at Norman and added, "It feels like we have two conflicting calls on our lives—to join WEC and to somehow keep the bookstore."

"But we're not sure," Bessie said. "Do you think we should close the bookstore? Could that really be what God wants us to do?"

Norman spoke before thinking through what he was about to say. "Of course not! Don't close it down.

There ought to be more of them—Christian book-stores scattered up and down the country."

From Colchester, Norman and Leslie traveled on to Chelmsford, twenty-two miles to the southwest. There they spoke at a meeting, after which Norman got into conversation with the Whybrows, who were WEC supporters. When Norman learned that they held a regular prayer meeting for WEC missionaries, he asked them to pray for new workers for the litera-ture project being developed in Colchester.

Within days of returning to WEC headquarters in London, Norman received two letters. The first was from Ken, who reported, "As we pray and think and dream, the vision keeps enlarging. We can see not only a chain of bookshops across the British Isles, but also a chain of bookstores throughout the Eng-lish-speaking world . . . and even in other countries where English is widely used. And more, we could become a service agency for the literature needs of missionary societies and the national church around the world. We have been doing this very thing in a limited way . . . now the whole world is our vision."

The second letter was from Fred Whybrow, who wrote to say that he and his wife felt called to sell their grocery business and move to Colchester to help Ken and Bessie Adams start a Christian Literature Cru-sade that would work under Norman's direction.

Norman smiled as he read Fred's letter. This was nothing he could have planned. The Christian Liter-ature Crusade had landed in his lap, and he felt it was the right step to take. Each of the eleven WEC centers they were establishing would offer a range of Christian literature. By November the Whybrow and Adams families were living and working together to expand their vision of using Christian literature throughout the United Kingdom and eventually around the world. Christians in twenty towns had already reached out to Norman to see if they could also have a Christian Literature Crusade ministry.

One by one, Christians from many denominations stepped forward to start more WEC centers, volunteering to work without pay, some using their own homes as the center. Centers also opened in Bristol, Cardiff, Macclesfield, Belfast, Nottingham, and Bournemouth, while the existing center in Glasgow was strengthened. By the start of the staff conference in January 1942, eight regional WEC centers were operating, each with its own story of faith.

Despite the war, WEC's overseas missionaries held firm, and two new mission fields, one on the Gold Coast of Africa and the other on the Caribbean island of Dominica, were opened. However, in February 1942 the Japanese captured the British colony of Singapore and took twenty-five thousand prisoners. The island nation contained Great Britain's major military base in Southeast Asia and the Southwest Pacific, and British Prime Minister Winston Churchill described its capture as the worst disaster of the war so far.

The capture of Singapore, however, was tempered by the news that in early May 1942 the United States, which had entered the war on the side of the

Allies six months before, had beaten the Japanese at the Battle of Midway in the Pacific. Soon afterward Germany suffered military setbacks at Stalingrad in the Soviet Union and at El Alamein in Egypt, though the war was far from over. The Allied victory at El Alamein came at a personal cost to Norman and Pauline. In July 1942, they received a telegram informing them their nephew George Barclay, the son of Gilbert and Dorothy, had been killed in action at El Alamein. George was twenty-two years old and a decorated fighter pilot.

A little over a year later, on September 30, 1943, Norman received news that his and Pauline's nephew Lionel Buxton had died from wounds he received while fighting in Sicily. Norman's heart went out to his sister-in-law Edith Buxton, who had now lost both her husband and her only son in the war.

As the war dragged on, the work of WEC continued to increase in the United Kingdom with two more centers opening, one in Birmingham and the other in Aberdeen, bringing the total number of centers to fourteen.

The following year, in March 1944, Norman attended the twenty-fifth anniversary of InterVarsity Fellowship (IVF), which had grown out of the original Cambridge Intercollegiate Christian Union meeting Norman had instigated in 1919. He was humbled to see how much the tiny organization he had helped found had grown. He addressed 320 student leaders from universities in England, the United States, Canada, New Zealand, Australia, and China. Norman was excited as he listened to the organization's plans to expand to other countries around the world, which included having branches in Muslim universities in the Middle East.

Two months later, in May 1944, Norman learned that Gilbert and Dorothy Barclay's twenty-seven-year-old son, Charles, had been killed fighting the Japanese in Kohima, India. Gilbert and Dorothy now had only one son, Richard, left.

In Europe, the tide of the war was beginning to turn. On Tuesday, June 6, 1944, a massive Allied invasion began at Normandy, France. The goal of the invasion was to liberate France from Nazi control, and from there begin an invasion of Germany.

A week after the invasion began in Normandy, Hitler unleashed a new weapon on Great Britain—the V1 jet-powered flying bomb, or Doodlebug as it was soon being called. The Doodlebug was unlike anything the world had ever seen. It was a self-propelled missile that could be launched from the ground rather than dropped from aircraft. At night, Doodlebugs began to rain down on London and the south of England, killing thousands of people and destroying over 200,000 homes, along with train stations, power stations, and bridges.

During October 1944, three of the four WEC houses in Upper Norwood were severely damaged by Doodlebugs. The only livable structure was the hostel at number 19 because it had been constructed with metal girders. Most of the WEC staff in London scattered to the regional centers while a cleanup crew began the process of setting the London houses back in order.

Through it all, the work of WEC continued. Norman visited the regional centers, grateful that the mission had felt led to spread its operations across the British Isles. As a result, despite the headquarters in London being severely damaged, all the staff had somewhere to go, and the work of the mission carried on.

On May 7, 1945, Germany surrendered and the war in Europe came to a halt. Then on September 2, 1945, almost six years after it began, the Second World War ended with the surrender of Japan.

Everyone in the United Kingdom was relieved when the fighting ended. It had been a brutal and bloody war fought on many battlefields around the world. Yet while the war had raged on, the work of WEC had continued to move forward. During the war years, the mission deployed 140 missionaries to serve around the world. At the start of the war, the mission's income had been 12,500 pounds, while at the close of the war that figure had risen to 38,000 pounds. As well, numerous WEC centers were scattered across the United Kingdom, and the Christian Literature Crusade (CLC) was flourishing.

Meanwhile, Norman noted another important change, which he explained in a letter to C.U.M.B. members. "I am convinced that this is supremely God's day of opportunity for the U.S.A. and that we ought to give all encouragement and sympathy to our American brethren. There is much more spiritual response there than here I am sorry to say, and there are great numbers of young people ready to go to various fields, and many missions have large sums of money for the purpose."

Norman eagerly anticipated the new things God might have in store for WEC.

Chapter 14

The Mother Field

Norman sat staring out the window as the propellers whirled, dragging the airplane forward. He was four days into his trip, and the droning propellers began lulling him to sleep. He was relieved that this flight would be nowhere near as long as the trip south from London. That flight had taken nearly twenty-four hours, including landing several times to refuel. This meant clambering out of the plane and waiting in a hot and stuffy airport building while men pumped in more fuel and readied the aircraft for the next leg of the journey. Norman had been glad when they landed at Leopoldville along the lower reaches of the Congo River. Despite the refueling stops, he was amazed at how fast he reached the Belgian Congo compared to the many weeks of travel by ship, riverboat, and overland trekking that he and Pauline had endured to reach the Congo on their first trip thirty years before.

After four days in Leopoldville visiting old friends and the leaders of missions working in the country, Norman was now on the next leg of his journey, a thousand-mile flight inland to Stanleyville. It was five days before Christmas 1949, and as they flew in a northeasterly direction toward the heart of Africa, Norman was able to see the Congo in a way he'd never seen it before—from above. The beauty below him was breathtaking. The lush, dense forests carpeted the hills and valleys, and among the trees he would catch a glimpse of the occasional road that to him looked like brown thread running through green cloth. He thought about all the WEC mission stations and local churches scattered among the lush, green covering on the ground.

As the aircraft approached Stanleyville, Norman looked forward to seeing some of the old workers again and meeting the many new missionaries who'd come through the London training program. Jack Scholes, who first came to the Belgian Congo in 1922 and worked alongside C.T. Studd, was now director of WEC's work in the Congo. He had replaced Jack Harrison in that position in 1945 followings Jack's sudden death from a tropical disease. Jack Scholes had arranged a five-month tour for Norman of the mission's work throughout the area.

After a six-hour flight, the airplane touched down on the red clay runway in Stanleyville. Norman gathered up his bags and climbed down the stairs onto the tarmac. Inside the small, crowded airport terminal he saw Jack Scholes waving at him. As the two men embraced, Norman thought how good it was to be back. Eighteen years had passed since his last visit to the Congo.

The two men spent the night in a guesthouse. The next day they got up early, loaded the Land Rover with mission supplies Jack had collected, and departed Stanleyville. They were headed 320 miles northeast to Wamba. Norman was enthralled to be driving through the Congo again. He jotted down notes as they went, describing the countryside as "amazingly beautiful. It is like driving through countless miles of parkland, the soft green and teeming vegetation right to the edges of the red-brown motor roads, tens of thousands of palm trees with their lovely waving fronds, from which Levers and others manufacture soap; and villages, villages everywhere, mud and bamboo huts of all sizes and shapes scattered among their groves of banana trees."

As the men drove up in the Land Rover, local Christians and missionaries ran to greet Norman and Jack, dancing and singing. By now it was dinnertime, and the two men were treated to a native feast. Afterward, Jack and Norman strolled past a well-kept garden. "That's God's Garden," Jack said. "I've written about it in the mission newsletter."

Norman nodded, recalling the article. The garden had been the community's idea. Every Thursday Christians from outlying small bush churches came to Wamba to tend it. They planted, hoed, weeded, and harvested rice, plantains, peanuts, and greens. These Christians considered it an honor to be able to work without wages, something Belgian government leaders in the area found difficult to understand. The produce the Christians grew was used to support their own Christian workers and feed students at the local WEC primary schools.

The next morning Norman and Jack climbed back into the Land Rover and made their way west toward Ibambi. Jack told Norman they would return to Wamba in a week and a half for the New Year's conference.

On the way to Ibambi the road became more twisted and overgrown. It passed through stretches of ancient forest still untouched by man on either side, where giant trees towered 150 feet or more.

Approaching Ibambi, Norman heard the sound of whistles and then watched as hundreds of shining faces emerged from village huts and tree groves. Girls, boys, women, and men all gathered around the Land Rover as it pulled to a halt under a huge flower arch set up over the road. The joyous crowd welcomed Norman, followed by a parade through the village and then speeches and feasting. As the welcome continued, Norman recognized old faces among the crowd and was introduced to many new schoolchildren and adult Bible school students.

The following morning Norman, accompanied by Jack, was shown around the mission facility. The buildings were twice as big as they had been when he last saw them, and most of them were now made of sturdy brick. The Bible school facility particularly impressed Norman. The combination dining/meeting hall was large enough to service the needs of 150 people. But it was the small brick bungalows that really caught Norman's attention. Each bungalow was built to house a married couple. This was something that had not been possible years before because women weren't considered important enough to educate. Now, Jack explained, couples were eager to come to the college and study together. Each man and woman had to pass a reading and writing test and be recommended by the local village church before being accepted into the institution. The couple would then live and study side by side, both taking the same tests and graduating after two years.

Norman was very impressed. He knew how hard this change would have been for the Congolese to accept. In most social situations a man would never eat in the company of a woman, but here they were, in the Bible school studying Scripture together and preparing and eating their meals as a group.

Jack chuckled as he told Norman about the Bible school's beginnings. "At the start, the school met with absolute opposition from the African church, and we 'opened' without a single student! But Jack Harrison had faith, and now we have many couples out at mission stations and twenty here training at the moment. We have enough applications to bring the number up to thirty next year, and the whole thing is paid for by the village churches—not a penny of foreign mission funds goes into this. This is what God has laid on their hearts and they give willingly to sustain it."

Norman smiled, thinking of his mother-in-law, Priscilla Studd, and her favorite Bible verse: "God loves a cheerful giver." How she would have loved to see the way the local village churches gave so enthusiastically to fund the Bible school.

The last time Norman had been in Ibambi, C.T. was alive and in control of the mission. Now he was buried in the village, and Norman visited his father-in-law's gravesite for the first time. As he stood beside the grave, he thought about all the changes that had taken place since he and Pauline said their final goodbyes to C.T. eighteen years earlier. The period following C.T.'s death had been tumultuous for Norman and the mission. For a while it looked like WEC might not survive, but Norman remembered the day he felt God challenge the staff in London to pray and believe that in the coming year ten new missionaries would be trained and sent to the Congo. Those prayers had been answered, and the ten new missionaries had been sent out between December 1931 and December 1932. They became known as "the Ten."

Following the sending out of the Ten, WEC's work began to flourish on mission field after mission field around the world. Norman was humbled by all God had done for the mission over the years. He had come to the Belgian Congo in 1920 happy to spend his days sharing the gospel with those who dwelt in the heart of Africa, but God had a different course for Norman's life. And now here he stood, next to his father-in-law's grave, serving as the general secretary of the mission C.T. had founded, a mission that was continuing to grow and flourish around the world.

A number of missionaries who made up the Ten were still serving in the Belgian Congo, and Norman was delighted to renew fellowship with some of them. In Ibambi, he was reunited with Frank Cripps and his wife, the former Lily Peckett. Frank and Harold Coleman were the first two of the Ten, and Lily had been the fourth. During his years in the Congo, Frank had taught himself to run a printing press, and he became an excellent printer. He handled WEC's printing needs, from New Testaments in various local languages to hymnals and teaching materials. He took Norman on a tour of the print shop, where he'd trained six local men to work alongside him. Working together they produced a constant stream of books and booklets from their simple treadle printing press, which Frank had ingeniously rigged to be powered from a gasoline engine. In fact, Frank told Norman, the standard of work they produced was so good that other missions were asking if they would print their materials.

Norman was impressed by all Frank had achieved and took great pleasure in informing him that the Christian Literature Crusade had used some of its profits from the sale of Christian literature to purchase a larger printing press for the print shop in Ibambi. The new press was already on its way to the Congo by ship.

As Christmas weekend 1949 approached, Christians from neighboring bush churches began arriving in Ibambi for the Christmas conference. A huge shelter consisting of support poles holding up a palm-frond roof was erected for the three thousand or so people expected to attend. Jack proudly told Norman that the conference meetings were all arranged and led by African workers and that the missionaries had to be invited by them to preach. Norman knew this was exactly what the missionaries had been working so hard to achieve. This was something that would have gladdened C.T.'s heart.

Norman was delighted to be one of the missionaries asked to speak at the conference. And when he stood to speak, he was relieved to discover he still remembered the Bangala language, much to the delight of the conference attendees.

The conference lasted four days. For Norman they were four days of beautiful singing, stirring preaching, and much Christian encouragement. Early on the last morning of the event, Norman witnessed another sign that the Congolese church was rising up to take control of its own destiny. Representatives of all of the small surrounding bush churches carried sealed wooden money boxes into the middle of a large circle. There they emptied the contents onto the ground one box at a time, where church elders counted how much money had been in each box. Clapping and shouting followed each tally as the amount was announced and written on a large chalkboard. Thousands of Congolese francs were raised,

and every bit of the money would be used by local
churches to help fund evangelists and pay for materials to build permanent church buildings.

Norman was still pondering the Ibambi Christmas conference when he and Jack set out to return to
Wamba for the New Year conference. In Wamba they
received another warm welcome. Twelve hundred
schoolchildren from the town and surrounding bush
schools were waiting for them. Accompanied by two
students playing cornets, they paraded around the
football field in their blue-and-white uniforms. It was
a sight Norman knew he would never forget.

In Wamba Norman met with the missionaries to
listen to their concerns and share in their victories. He
was particularly impressed with the group of female
Sunday school teachers headed by WEC missionary
Muriel Harman. Three hundred Christian women
would meet in small groups once a week where they
were trained to teach Sunday school lessons using
materials Muriel had written and Frank's team had
printed. The women were shown how to teach Bible
verse memorization, lead singing, and disciple the
children they reached with the gospel. Norman was
delighted to learn that just a few years earlier most of
these women in training had never heard the gospel
themselves.

While in Wamba, Norman enjoyed meeting with
the forty Congolese evangelists and their wives who
worked in and around the outlying area.

On January 8, 1950, Colin and Ina Buckley accompanied Norman one hundred miles south to visit a

church planted among the Babari tribe. On arrival at the main church center, Norman learned that it served eighteen other bush churches. There he met Malibatu, the fifty-year-old man who led the church. Malibatu asked Norman to preach during the upcoming weekend conference, in which about five hundred Christians from across the region were expected to participate. Norman gladly accepted the invitation.

As the first day of the conference approached, Norman watched as local Christians arrive, some carrying little children and others carrying baskets and bunches of plantains. Norman learned that some of the attendees had trudged fifty to seventy-five miles through the forest to get there. Norman was amazed that despite the distance they had traveled, they all arrived enthusiastically singing gospel songs with an air of expectancy for what God would do among them.

Norman preached during the Sunday service. The crowd sang joyfully, and then he delivered a simple sermon proclaiming the gospel. At the end of the service, eight people responded to the message and gave their lives to Jesus Christ.

Much to Norman's delight, early the following morning Malibatu poked his head through the guest hut window and announced, "I have not slept this night. God has done a mighty work. All through the night people were coming to me, including several of the evangelists, saying that God had struck their hearts yesterday and they must put things right with Him. There is much confession and repenting going on in the village."

Later that morning, his heart full of joy over the way God had blessed the conference, Norman returned to Wamba with Colin and Ina. From Wamba, Norman and Jack set out on more of their grand tour of mission outposts. This time they headed south to Opienge and the mission center among the Balumbi tribe. At Opienge they were welcomed by Miss Roupell, the mission's longest-serving worker. She had joined the mission in the Congo in 1916 and thirty-three years later was still there. Ivor and Rose Davies were also stationed there. Ivor was called Mr. Ten by the Congolese, as he'd been the tenth person of the Ten. His wife, Rose, had been Rose Sore, the ninth person of the Ten sent out. The couple traveled to the Congo together, and along the way love blossomed and they were married in 1935. Zamu, a lame evangelist also lived at Opienge. He was just as fiery as he'd been when he stood over C.T.'s coffin and vowed to take the gospel to the Balumbi people. For Norman it was wonderful to see them all, English and Congolese, working together, especially since local Christians faced so much opposition. The area around Opienge was well-known for its witchcraft, and many Christians were tortured because they challenged the spiritual authority of the witches.

Norman's trip with Jack continued on week after week as they visited new mission stations and older established ones. Along the way Norman witnessed how Winnie Davies was saving many babies in her maternity home, and how Arthur and Irene Scott, along with an American couple, Will and Rhodie

Dawn, were overseeing a leprosy village caring for thirteen hundred people.

In Egbita Norman learned about a native evangelist named Solomono. He had been present in Ibambi when C.T. died. In response to watching C.T.'s death, Solomono, an old man himself at the time, vowed he would follow C.T.'s lead and live among a strange people and share the gospel with them. He left Ibambi and settled among the Mejes tribe, where he lived for seventeen years before dying and being buried at the Egbita mission station. Now, as a result of Solomono's effort, twelve bush churches were in the area, and 250 local Christians attended the conference, at which Norman spoke in Egbita.

By mid-March 1950, Norman was in Poko. On his arrival a letter was waiting for him from Pauline. He tore it open, anxious to read the news from his wife. Sadly, the letter contained some bad news. The month before, on February 13, at the age of seventy-one, Norman's old friend Rees Howells had died. Norman mourned his friend's passing and thanked God for leading Rees to him back in 1928 at the Keswick convention. No other man, aside from C.T. Studd, had had as great a spiritual impact on Norman's life than Rees Howells.

In Poko Norman enjoyed fellowship with Vernon Willson, the sixth missionary of the Ten. He was also delighted to reunite with Lilian Dennis, the nurse he and Pauline had traveled with to the Congo thirty years before. In Poko about five hundred Christians from the more than thirty outlying churches in the area showed up for the conference. Vernon explained to Norman that this was somewhat fewer than usual because the planting season had already begun.

Norman and Jack spent the last week of their grand tour at Nala, a place that held many good memories for Norman. It was where he and Pauline had first served after their arrival as missionaries in the Belgian Congo in 1920. It was also where Norman had come face-to-face with his tall, gaunt, bushy-bearded father-in-law, C.T. Studd, for the first time. C.T. had welcomed Norman enthusiastically to the family and to the mission field.

Nala also held some dark memories for Norman. It was where Noel Grubb, their infant son, had died and was buried. And it was also where Norman, who came to Africa thinking he knew so much about being a missionary and running a mission station, learned that he actually knew very little about either of those things.

To complete his time in the Congo, Norman attended the last two days of the first African Leaders Conference, where 150 church leaders, evangelists, and their wives met to talk about the steps they needed to take to become independent of foreign missionaries. For Norman, as the general secretary of WEC, such talk was music to his ears. As European missionaries, he and Pauline had come to sow the seeds of the gospel among those living in the heart of the African continent. They had done their part and had seen many converts. Congolese Christians had begun gathering to pray and fellowship and encourage one another, and now those gatherings had grown into strong, independent, national churches. Norman wished his father-in-law could have been there to witness and savor the moment.

Following his visit to the Belgian Congo, Norman traveled on to neighboring Rwanda, where he spent two weeks before returning home in late May 1950. As he flew back to England, he pondered the many good things he would be able to report once he arrived back at WEC headquarters. In the next edition of the mission newsletter, Norman wrote,

> "Great is the Lord and greatly to be praised." I return to the homeland with a stronger confirmation than I have ever had in my life of the simple fact that the gospel of Christ *is* the power of God unto salvation. I knew the heart of Africa in its days of total darkness; now I have seen the marvellous transformations, not of the outward—clothes, education, money— but of what clothes and cash, and the laws of the state, can never produce; the heart made pure through the blood of Christ, the evil habits destroyed, the life lived in the love and beauty of the Spirit in the happy service of God and man. "The Heart of Africa Mission," as it was originally called, is the mother field of the WEC, God's pattern, we believe, for all those younger fields, now twenty in number, to which God has sent our fellow-Crusaders.

Chapter 15

A New Challenge

Following Norman's return to Great Britain, he and Pauline made a long trip to the United States, where they settled their youngest son, Daniel, into university at Wheaton College in Illinois. Norman continued to be amazed by the openness of Americans to the gospel. Everywhere he and Pauline went, they seemed to see new churches being built. A young evangelist named Billy Graham was taking the country by storm, holding crusade meetings to proclaim the gospel across the country. During September the year before, Billy Graham began a series of crusade meetings in Los Angeles. The meetings were held in a circus tent erected on a vacant lot that held six thousand people. The crusade was supposed to run for three weeks, but so many people showed up that it was extended to eight. By the end of the crusade, 350,000 people had come to hear Billy Graham preach, and over 3,000 people had become Christians. When Norman read about this, he could not imagine such a thing happening in England.

Elsewhere, WEC opened new mission fields in Japan, Uruguay, France, Borneo, and Sumatra. Since the end of World War II, large numbers of young men and women had answered the call to go and evangelize in new areas.

Back in England in 1951, Norman took the opportunity to do something he'd wanted to do since learning of the death of Rees Howells—write a biography of his old friend. Norman was convinced that Rees and his team of intercessors had done more to turn the tide of World War II in favor of the Allies than just about anyone or anything else. Through telling Rees's story, he wanted to introduce people to the man who'd had such a significant impact on him personally and on the world at large. It was a big project tracing Rees's life from his days as a tin miner in Wales in the 1890s through his conversion in America, his marriage, his call to Africa, and then his return back to Wales. As he wrote, Norman stayed for long periods in a house opposite the Bible college in Wales, sifting through notes, journals, and index cards filled with information. He also interviewed Rees's widow, Lizzy, and their only son, Samuel, along with many of the older college staff.

Once the Rees Howells biography was completed and sent off to the publisher, Norman embarked upon a year-long tour of Australia, New Zealand, Indonesia, Siam, and India. Everywhere he went he preached to native groups and met with missionaries to support them in any way he could. During the long trip, Pauline wrote to tell him that their oldest son, Paul, and his wife, Aline, were no longer happy together. The couple had two young children, Sandy and Nicholas. Norman was sad to hear of their marital struggles and began to pray for them.

Good news also arrived from home. The biography, titled *Rees Howells Intercessor*, had been published and was selling well. A Mrs. Wood from the United States had read the book and now wanted permission to print twenty thousand additional copies to be given away to American students. Also, as part of her coronation, Queen Elizabeth II had awarded a number of knighthoods. One of those knighthoods had gone to Norman's brother Kenneth for his service with the Church Missionary Society. Norman wondered if he would ever get used to calling his younger brother "Sir Kenneth."

Regretfully, Kenneth and Norman's older brother, Harold, had not done so well. Never fully recovering from his ordeal during World War I, Harold had spent most of his life traveling and living between Switzerland, the United Kingdom, and South Africa. In April 1954, while on a voyage back to South Africa, sixty-one-year-old Harold suffered a heart attack and died and was buried at sea. Now only three Grubb siblings were still alive. In 1955, Norman's sister, Violet, accepted the prestigious position as principal of Salisbury Training College, which trained British schoolteachers.

Also in 1955, on August 2, Norman celebrated his sixtieth birthday. He spent the day attending the annual conference of the Christian Literature Crusade. Fifty workers from CLC were present, and the more he listened to their reports, the more excited he became. CLC bookshops in Great Britain had sold 260,000 Christian books during the previous year, and the organization was expanding into Korea, the Philippines, Brazil, Austria, and Colombia. Trevor Shaw, a New Zealand journalist working with CLC, had a vision to start producing simply worded Christian magazines suitable for people who were just learning to read. Already two of these magazines had been produced and distributed, one in Nigeria and the other in French West Africa. The approach had proved popular, and Christian magazines for the West Indies and Latin America were already in production. Norman was excited to learn of the many ministry opportunities opening up for CLC. He left the conference feeling energized and ready for a new challenge.

That challenge came a year later in a form neither Norman nor Pauline had anticipated. Their son Paul's marriage had continued to deteriorate, and by 1956 their daughter-in-law Aline had deserted the family, leaving Paul with two small children to raise. The task proved too much for him, and he asked Norman and Pauline to take over as the children's guardians. Norman and Pauline hadn't imagined themselves playing the role of parents again, but as they prayed about the situation, they felt it was the right thing to do. And so, they took on the guardianship of nine-year-old Sandra and six-year-old Nicholas. Norman knew that taking on this responsibility was a big sacrifice, particularly for Pauline, who was looking forward to spending more time traveling with him. Now she would need to stay home with the children. Nonetheless, the two of them committed themselves to the task.

During the summer of 1956, Norman was asked to co-lead WEC's work in North America for three years. He had been struck by the amazing opportunities for Christian work and missionary recruitment in the United States since the end of World War II. Since no one knew how much longer it might last, he decided to accept the position. This meant that he and Pauline would have to apply to the courts for permission to take their two grandchildren to the United States with them. As part of the arrangement, their thirty-two-year-old daughter, Priscilla, agreed to go with them so that she could be someone closer to the children's parents' ages.

It was difficult for Norman to leave his mother behind. She was now ninety-three years old and in poor health. He was glad his sister, Violet, lived not too far away from their mother and was able to help her.

The Grubb family—Norman, Pauline, Priscilla, Sandra, and Nicholas—set sail from Southampton on April 11, 1957, aboard the SS *United States*, bound for New York. After a stop in La Havre, France, across the English Channel, the ship headed west into the Atlantic. The trip was fast. The *United States* was a newly designed superliner that had already set a world record by crossing the Atlantic Ocean in fewer than four days. Everything aboard the vessel was new and modern, and Norman kept a sharp eye on Sandra and Nicholas as they explored. The children especially liked using the ship's elevators that took them down far below deck.

The family arrived safely in New York on April 16 and, after spending a night in New York City, boarded a train for the trip south to Fort Washington, Pennsylvania. Alfred Ruscoe had worked tirelessly since arriving in North America twenty-three years before. As a result, WEC had a number of thriving centers across Canada and the United States. Norman was particularly looking forward to seeing the new combined WEC-CLC headquarters in Fort Washington. As the diesel locomotive sped pulling the train along, he told the children the story of how the mission came to own the huge property to which they were headed.

Sandra and Nicholas loved hearing how, during the American Revolution, George Washington had camped out with his troops at Camp Hill just before they marched to Valley Forge for the winter of 1777. Norman explained that 105 years later in 1882, John and Sarah Fell, a wealthy Philadelphia couple, had chosen Camp Hill as the site for their summer home. On the site they had built a stone mansion that looked like a Scottish castle. It had forty-three rooms and thirteen fireplaces and was surrounded by seventy acres of woodland. After the Fells died, the place was turned into a military academy, but the venture failed, and the property was abandoned in 1948. Over the next three years the old mansion was almost completely wrecked by thieves and vandals. Every window in the place was broken, and the copper pipes and electrical lights were ripped out. Homeless squatters had left piles of junk inside.

The owner put the mansion and outbuildings, along with the seventy acres of land, up for sale for $150,000 in 1951. When she learned that a missionary group was thinking of buying the property, she reduced the price to $60,000. Money flowed in from friends of WEC to cover the purchase price, and the mission took possession of the place. The buildings underwent renovation and restoration. Before long the property was a busy and overcrowded missionary center.

That was why Norman was grateful that some mission-minded friends had offered the Grubb family both a fully furnished home to live in near Camp Hill and a car to drive. The privacy of their own home would help bind the "new" family together as Norman and Pauline moved into this new phase of their lives. After the move to Pennsylvania, Pauline, now sixty-three years old, became ill and needed the rest and relative quiet the house afforded. With Pauline's health issues, Norman was grateful that their daughter, Priscilla, had agreed to emigrate with them and help with the children.

In January 1958 as the Grubbs adjusted to their first winter together in the United States, Norman received word that his mother had died. While he was sad that he would never see her on earth again, he thanked God for her long life and godly influence on so many people, including him.

With his family settled in Pennsylvania, Norman continued his book writing and world travel. He continued to be amazed at the openness of Christians in the United States to missions as he spoke in churches and other venues around the country. He did, however, encounter a recurring problem. As he got older, Norman spoke faster and mumbled more, which, coupled with his strong British accent, made it difficult for him to be understood when he spoke at large gatherings. He felt more at ease in small fellowship meetings and house churches, where he could talk slower and more informally as he encouraged Christians to support missions.

The year 1960 was a big one for Norman. His youngest son, Daniel, married Rose Callan on June 4, and on June 30, the Congo became independent from Belgium. Norman hoped that things would go well for the newly independent country, although he saw some signs that concerned him that things might not go as smoothly as hoped. As various political factions vied for power, it seemed the new Congolese government was in danger of collapsing.

A little over a month after the Congo gained its independence, Norman turned sixty-five years old. While most men retired at that age, Norman was not about to do that, and the spring of 1961 found him busy preparing for the first international leaders conference that was about to be held in Kilcreggan, near Glasgow, in Scotland. At the conference, sixty WEC and CLC leaders from around the world met for a month to set the course of the mission for the next ten years. Norman was thrilled to see a younger generation rising up to embrace the same principles upon which C.T. Studd had founded the mission: sacrifice, faith, holiness, and fellowship. In fact, Norman decided his next book would be on those four principles. Together the leaders looked at the thousand missionaries they had working in forty mission fields and their nine sending bases and asked God to guide them forward as individuals and as an organization. Several decisions made during the conference affected Norman. The first was that going forward, WEC North America should be led by an executive committee of seven men chosen by the staff. Norman felt this was a good step, and it would also free him up to do more of the small house group preaching and teaching that he loved to do. Of course, he was still General Secretary of the mission, though that title was changed to International Secretary during the conference to reflect WEC's international reach.

After the conference was over, Norman spent much of his time speaking and guiding the mission on an international level while remaining based in Fort Washington. In 1963, he was asked to serve another three-year term as international secretary, which he agreed to do. Directing WEC International

turned out to be one of the most difficult times that
Norman ever faced. The mission field in the Belgian Congo was the cradle of WEC. The mission was
founded there. It was also where Norman and Pauline started their missionary journey and where other
leaders in the organization began their service. By
1963, Norman knew he'd been right to be concerned
about the country's stability in 1960 when the Congo
became independent. The new government soon collapsed, and the country was now trapped in an endless round of civil war and violence, which made the
work of missionaries there difficult and dangerous.

In 1964 a fierce new rebellion emerged centered
around Stanleyville. It began spreading into northeast Congo, where WEC's missionaries served. The
rebellion was carried out by a group calling themselves Simbas. They had a reputation for brutality
against other Congolese and missionaries alike. At
the end of 1964, devasting news reached Norman.
The Simbas had captured a group of WEC missionaries from Ibambi and the outlying stations, including the missionary doctor Helen Roseveare, along
with other white missionaries, and Catholic priests
and nuns. The Simbas were threatening to kill them
all. Norman and WEC leaders prayed fervently for
the situation and the safety of all those captured.
Then, on the last day of the year, Norman was able
to breathe a sigh of relief. News reached him that
the captured missionaries had been liberated and
would soon be flown out of the country. But his relief
was tempered by the fact that the Simbas had killed

numerous priests and nuns and thirty-one of the captured missionaries, at least two of whom were WEC missionaries.

In 1966, Norman's post as international secretary came up for reappointment. Norman felt that his days leading WEC were at an end, and he recommended Len Moules, his old friend from his days in the Belgian Congo, for the position. From the Belgian Congo, Len had spent several years doing missionary work in the Himalayan mountains of Northern India before taking over leadership of WEC in the United Kingdom when Norman moved to the United States.

Len was duly appointed to the position of international secretary. On New Year's Eve 1965, for the first time in forty-five years, Norman and Pauline Grubb were free of their leadership responsibilities in WEC. Many people congratulated them on their retirement, but retirement was the furthest thing from Norman's mind.

Chapter 16

An Astonishing Legacy

On New Year's Day 1966, Norman, now seventy years old, contemplated how many more years he might have to live. His father had died at seventy-six and his mother at ninety-six. But one thing he and Pauline agreed upon: however long they lived, they would both make each day count for God. Norman was spurred on by one of C.T. Studd's famous quotes: "Let us not glide through this world and then slip quietly into heaven, without having blown the trumpet loud and long for our Redeemer, Jesus Christ. Let us see to it that the devil will hold a thanksgiving service in hell, when he gets the news of our departure from the field of battle."

Now that he was free of his leadership roles, Norman turned his attention to something he loved—teaching the Bible in small group settings. He began traveling throughout the United States teaching and praying with others. Many of those who hosted Norman asked him to put in writing and publish his teachings, which he did in a series of short books.

Each year he made at least one trip back to England, mainly at the invitation of WEC or CLC to participate in conferences or strategy meetings. Norman loved to tell people about the beginnings of each organization and how God had been faithful to them.

While back in England in 1967, Norman learned that the Greater London Council had plans for the WEC houses and the others on the street. All the homes on Highland Road were old, and a number of them had been damaged by German bombs during World War II. Stopgap repairs were made to some houses at the time while others were left derelict. It was time, the council decided, to tear them all down and replace them with new housing. Number 17 Highland Road was one of the homes the council wanted to tear down, along with eight houses WEC now owned. Number 17 had been C.T. Studd's personal home and had later served as the headquarters house for WEC. It was much later passed down to Norman and Pauline as an inheritance. While technically they owned the place, Norman and Pauline decide to give the old Studd family home to the mission. That way it could become part of the deal that the Greater London Council wanted to strike with WEC.

Len Moules told Norman that he was negotiating with the council, arguing that all the WEC houses formed a community and it would be difficult for the mission to again find that many houses for sale in the same area. The council agreed and offered to buy a suitable replacement property for WEC. They settled on buying Bulstrode Park and House, a large red-brick Victorian manor house set on seventy acres of land situated on the western outskirts of London. The property was worth 150,000 pounds, ten times what WEC had paid for all their houses on Highland Road. Norman was astounded when he saw photos of Bulstrode Park. The manor house was huge, consisting of 115 rooms. It would be a perfect place to hold retreats and accommodate missionaries visiting from all over the world.

On his return to Fort Washington, Norman began his next venture, writing an autobiography. He called the book *Once Caught, No Escape: My Life Story,* and it was published by Lutterworth Press in London in 1969.

As Norman grew older, he kept a rigorous pace of traveling and speaking. Pauline stayed behind at their home in Fort Washington, with Priscilla helping her.

Inevitably, as time passed, people Norman had been linked with in earlier years began to die. His brother-in-law, Gilbert Barclay, had died in 1970. Four years later, both Pauline's sister Grace and her husband, David Munro, died. Norman began to wonder how much longer he would have Pauline around. Her health was beginning to fail, and she suffered from a bleeding ulcer, for which she eventually underwent surgery. Susie Wheeler, an old friend from WEC England, offered to come to Pennsylvania to help take care of Pauline, freeing Norman to continue traveling and speaking.

More of Norman's family and fellow missionaries died, including Pauline's sister Edith Buxton in 1977 and Len Moules the following year. Still, Norman continued his ministry. He turned eighty-five in 1980, the same year in which his brother Kenneth died, as well as his sister-in-law Dorothy Barclay.

For a man of eighty-five, Norman remained in good health, except for his old knee injury. That knee was now riddled with arthritis, making it difficult for him to get on and off airplanes, and carrying his suitcase was exhausting. To his delight, his granddaughter Sandra, who was now thirty-three years old, came back to live with them. She had recently recommitted her life to God. Sandra felt strongly that because of her grandfather's arthritic knee she should drive him from place to place from now on, so that he would not have to fly. The only problem was, neither of them owned a car.

Within days of Sandra's offer, a check for ten thousand dollars arrived in the mail. The money had been left to Norman by an elderly woman whom he visited from time to time. He took the money and bought a Volkswagen, in which he and Sandra traveled from Florida to Maine. Sometimes the "small" groups Norman spoke to were so large that the hosts would set up an event tent on the lawn where the meeting was being held.

In early September 1981, Norman and Sandra embarked upon a three-month tour of the Midwest. They had just gotten started on the trip when word reached Norman that Pauline had died. They turned around and headed for home to arrange her funeral. Norman grieved his loss. Still, he knew this day had been coming, and he believed that Pauline was now waiting for him in heaven, where he would soon join her. Following Pauline's funeral, Norman continued traveling and speaking, with Sandra at his side to help.

In 1985 Norman's sister, Violet, died. Now, all his siblings, along with Pauline's sisters and their husbands, were dead. Norman was glad he got along so well with younger people, as there were fewer people his age to relate to.

In August 1985 Norman returned from a speaking tour to discover that Sandra had arranged a big celebration for his ninetieth birthday. Seventy of Norman's friends gathered from near and far to honor him. Norman was grateful for everyone who came and thankful he was able to once more spend time with friends.

Two years later, Norman was shocked when Sandra informed him she had been diagnosed with lung cancer. She was just forty years old, and together they had driven to each of forty-eight contiguous states, speaking to and praying for people as they went. Norman realized that this period of his life was coming to a close. Still, he comforted himself with the fact that he received hundreds of letters a year, with many letter writers seeking his spiritual advice. Norman was thankful that he could still write thoughtful replies to the letters. He was also encouraged by the way WEC and CLC were thriving.

At the beginning of 1990, Norman was visiting his friends Paige and Tom Prewitt in Jackson, Mississippi, when he became seriously ill. He was admitted to the hospital and diagnosed with pneumonia and a stomach ulcer. He was hospitalized for nearly a month, gaining a little strength each day, before being discharged into the Prewitts' care. After the hospital stay he could walk only short distances with the aid of a walker. Slowly he resumed some of his old activities. He hadn't been strong enough to deal with his mail while in the hospital and found 150 letters waiting for him when he was discharged.

When Norman was strong enough, he returned home to Fort Washington, where Sandra was very ill. He clung to the hope that she would be healed. He hired a day nurse to tend to him and Sandra, and many friends of the family took turns staying in their home to help out. Sadly, Sandra died on October 2, 1991. Upset that she had died while he still lived, Norman wept for three days following her death.

Following Sandra's death, Norman's health began to decline until he could no longer walk at all. Suspended over his bed was a sling, which his nurses used to help him get out of bed and into his favorite chair and then back again when he tired. Although his body was slowly wasting away, Norman's mind remained sharp, and he continued to do what he could from his bed.

On August 2, 1993, Norman celebrated his ninety-eighth birthday. By now he was very weak, and the only thing he was able to do was feed himself. He hated that he could no longer reply individually to every letter he received. Instead, he resorted to a duplicated letter, which his daughter, Priscilla, sent out for him. After his birthday Norman wrote, "I hate writing just these present glorious facts, and not touching the exact needed reply to most of your letters. At 98 years, and with many limitations that come with age, this is my best. You are all ever in my thoughts and prayers to our Heavenly Father. I thank you for your gifts of love that you all continue to send my way. Your letters and visits bring much joy."

From his bed Norman used his last reserves of energy to write a new foreword for his father-in-law C.T. Studd's book, *Rescue Shop Within a Yard of Hell*. With the foreword completed, on December 15, 1993, Norman died. His last words were, "Abba, Abba take me, please take me."

A week later, Dr. Daniel Grubb, Norman and Pauline's youngest son, officiated at his father's funeral at the George Washington Memorial Park Cemetery in Plymouth Meeting, Pennsylvania.

Norman Grubb left behind an astonishing legacy. He led WEC through a crisis and molded it into a powerful international missionary organization. He combined WEC and CLC, the latter of which he cofounded, to have over two thousand full-time staff on fifty-five mission fields, with Koreans, Indians,

Africans, and Latin Americans joining together as coworkers. Norman also cofounded InterVarsity Fellowship of Evangelical Unions, which over the years spawned like-minded unions in countries around the world that serve tens of thousands of Christian university students each year. He also authored forty-five books and booklets—including, *C.T. Studd, Cricketer and Pioneer,* published in 1933, and *Rees Howells Intercessor,* published in 1952—that have remained strong sellers over the eighty-five and sixty-six years, respectively, since they were first published.

Buxton, Edith. *Reluctant Missionary*. Fort Washington, PA: Christian Literature Crusade, 1968.

Dinnen, Stewart. *Faith on Fire: Norman Grubb and the Building of WEC*. Fearn, UK: Christian Focus Publications, 1997.

Grubb, Norman. *After C.T. Studd*. Grand Rapids: Zondervan, 1946.

———. *C.T. Studd: Cricketer and Pioneer*. London: The Religious Tract Society, 1933.

———. *Leap of Faith*. Fort Washington, PA: Christian Literature Crusade, 1962.

———. *Mighty through God: The Life of Edith Moules*. London: Lutterworth Press, 1951.

———. *A Mighty Work of the Spirit*. London: Studd Press, 1950.

———. *My Dear C.U.M.B.* Bloomington, IN: Author House, 2006.

———. *Once Caught, No Escape: My Life Story*. London: Lutterworth Press, 1969.

———. *Successor to C.T. Studd: The Story of Jack Harrison*. London: Lutterworth Press, 1949.

————. *With C.T. Studd in Congo Forests*. Grand Rapids: Zondervan, 1946.

Grubb, Sir Kenneth. *Crypts of Power: An Autobiography*. London: Hodder and Stoughton, 1971.

Roseveare, Helen. *Give Me This Mountain: An Autobiography*. London, InterVarsity, 1966.

Vincent, Eileen. *C.T. Studd and Priscilla: United to Fight for Jesus*. Bromley, Kent: Kingsway Publications, 1988.

WEC Archives. Special thank you to Fiona Adams for her effort granting us access and guiding us to the relevant WEC and Heart of Africa Mission newsletters.

Janet and Geoff Benge are a husband and wife writing team with more than thirty years of writing experience. Janet is a former elementary school teacher. Geoff holds a degree in history. Originally from New Zealand, the Benges spent ten years serving with Youth With A Mission. They have two daughters, Laura and Shannon, and an adopted son, Lito. They make their home in the Orlando, Florida, area.

Also from Janet and Geoff Benge...

More adventure-filled biographies for ages 10 to 100!

Christian Heroes: Then and Now

Gladys Aylward: The Adventure of a Lifetime • 978-1-57658-019-6
Nate Saint: On a Wing and a Prayer • 978-1-57658-017-2
Hudson Taylor: Deep in the Heart of China • 978-1-57658-016-5
Amy Carmichael: Rescuer of Precious Gems • 978-1-57658-018-9
Eric Liddell: Something Greater Than Gold • 978-1-57658-137-7
Corrie ten Boom: Keeper of the Angels' Den • 978-1-57658-136-0
William Carey: Obliged to Go • 978-1-57658-147-6
George Müller: Guardian of Bristol's Orphans • 978-1-57658-145-2
Jim Elliot: One Great Purpose • 978-1-57658-146-9
Mary Slessor: Forward into Calabar • 978-1-57658-148-3
David Livingstone: Africa's Trailblazer • 978-1-57658-153-7
Betty Greene: Wings to Serve • 978-1-57658-152-0
Adoniram Judson: Bound for Burma • 978-1-57658-161-2
Cameron Townsend: Good News in Every Language • 978-1-57658-164-3
Jonathan Goforth: An Open Door in China • 978-1-57658-174-2
Lottie Moon: Giving Her All for China • 978-1-57658-188-9
John Williams: Messenger of Peace • 978-1-57658-256-5
William Booth: Soup, Soap, and Salvation • 978-1-57658-258-9
Rowland Bingham: Into Africa's Interior • 978-1-57658-282-4
Ida Scudder: Healing Bodies, Touching Hearts • 978-1-57658-285-5
Wilfred Grenfell: Fisher of Men • 978-1-57658-292-3
Lillian Trasher: The Greatest Wonder in Egypt • 978-1-57658-305-0
Loren Cunningham: Into All the World • 978-1-57658-199-5
Florence Young: Mission Accomplished • 978-1-57658-313-5
Sundar Singh: Footprints Over the Mountains • 978-1-57658-318-0
C.T. Studd: No Retreat • 978-1-57658-288-6
Rachel Saint: A Star in the Jungle • 978-1-57658-337-1
Brother Andrew: God's Secret Agent • 978-1-57658-355-5
Clarence Jones: Mr. Radio • 978-1-57658-343-2
Count Zinzendorf: Firstfruit • 978-1-57658-262-6
John Wesley: The World His Parish • 978-1-57658-382-1
C. S. Lewis: Master Storyteller • 978-1-57658-385-2
David Bussau: Facing the World Head-on • 978-1-57658-415-6
Jacob DeShazer: Forgive Your Enemies • 978-1-57658-475-0
Isobel Kuhn: On the Roof of the World • 978-1-57658-497-2
Elisabeth Elliot: Joyful Surrender • 978-1-57658-513-9
D. L. Moody: Bringing Souls to Christ • 978-1-57658-552-8
Paul Brand: Helping Hands • 978-1-57658-536-8
Dietrich Bonhoeffer: In the Midst of Wickedness • 978-1-57658-713-3

Heroes of History

Available in paperback, e-book, and audiobook formats.
Unit Study Curriculum Guides are available for many biographies.
www.HeroesThenAndNow.com

CHRISTIAN HEROES: THEN & NOW are available in paperback, e-book, and audiobook formats, with more coming soon!

www.HeroesThenAndNow.com